MY PEERLESS STORY

FOOTPRINTS SERIES

Jane Errington, Editor

The life stories of individual women and men who were participants in interesting events help nuance larger historical narratives, at times reinforcing those narratives, at other times contradicting them. The Footprints series introduces extraordinary Canadians, past and present, who have led fascinating and important lives at home and throughout the world.

The series includes primarily original manuscripts but may consider the English-language translation of works that have already appeared in another language. The editor of the series welcomes inquiries from authors. If you are in the process of completing a manuscript that you think might fit into the series, please contact her, care of McGill-Queen's University Press, 1010 Sherbrooke Street West, Suite 1720, Montreal, QC, H3A 2R7.

MY PEERLESS STORY

It Starts with the Collar

ALVIN CRAMER SEGAL

McGill-Queen's University Press

Montreal & Kingston • London • Chicago

ISBN 978-0-7735-5016-2 (cloth)
ISBN 978-0-7735-5017-9 (ePDF)
ISBN 978-0-7735-5018-6 (ePUB)

Legal deposit second quarter 2017
Bibliothèque nationale du Québec

Printed in Canada on acid-free paper.

McGill-Queen's University Press acknowledges the support of the Canada Council for the Arts for our publishing program. We also acknowledge the financial support of the Government of Canada through the Canada Book Fund for our publishing activities.

Library and Archives Canada Cataloguing in Publication

Segal, Alvin Cramer, 1933–, author
    My Peerless story: it starts with the collar / Alvin Cramer Segal.

(Footprints series; 24)
Includes index.
Issued in print and electronic formats.
ISBN 978-0-7735-5016-2 (hardcover). – ISBN 978-0-7735-5017-9 (ePDF). – ISBN 978-0-7735-5018-6 (ePUB)

    1. Segal, Alvin Cramer, 1933–. 2. Peerless Clothing (Firm) – History. 3. Men's clothing industry – Canada – History. 4. Tailoring – Canada – History. 5. Jewish businesspeople – Canada – Biography. 6. Businesspeople – Canada – Biography. 7. Success in business. I. Title. II. Series: Footprints series; 24

HD9940.C32S44 2017   338.4'7687092   C2017-901162-6
                                                    C2017-901163-4

This book was typeset by Marquis Interscript in 11/14 Sabon.

*This book is dedicated to
my three children and eight grandchildren,
who I probably haven't told enough – but love very dearly*

Contents

Contents

Figures

Acknowledgments

I felt I had to tell my story. I wrote this book to explain how and why the traditional men's suit industry changed dramatically over the last sixty-five years and relate how my business instincts required me to be out in the world and approach every level of government (federal, provincial, and municipal). As a businessman, I had to be aware of the community as well as understand how my company fit in the global environment. I also needed to be able to communicate with every employee at every level. You can't just sit in your ivory tower. Success doesn't happen by accident.

I hope, by reading this book, young people will be encouraged to undertake their own business ventures. I didn't have a particular goal in mind when I started working other than to keep my job; that led me to keep improving step by step. My theory of having a long-range plan that changes every day has always worked to my advantage, enabling me to recognize and seize opportunities at the right moment. Another key factor to my success has been that I surrounded myself with so many good people in business and in my personal life.

It took me several years to write this book, and I must thank those who kept me going and encouraged me to take the book to different levels, including my cousin Rosie Pearson. It couldn't have been completed without their help. My family and friends and many colleagues took the time to read and review chapters, and gave helpful advice and valuable suggestions. A special thank you to my executive assistant, Shadia Daccache, who pulled all the loose ends together. Thank you all.

Foreword

Alvin Segal is probably best known for his wonderful philanthropic activities. He is also much respected for his successful efforts to lobby governments and other public bodies in the interests and defence of the garment-manufacturing industry in Canada. Somewhat less known, perhaps diminished by the passage of time, are his early successes in revolutionizing the technology of tailored men's garment construction and production.

Once upon a time, in the days before Alvin, the construction and production of tailored garments were driven by fashion designers and tailors, whose artistic inclinations added a certain mystique to the enterprise and thereby created a shield against the critical interventions of industrial engineers and production managers. There was much hand work, not enough efficiency, and high costs.

Along came young Alvin, perhaps still wet behind the ears, untutored in the mysteries of tailoring and very much the iconoclast. With a clear and questioning mind, he saw better ways and had the tenacity to overcome the entrenched culture. The end result was that he created an engineered tailored garment of equal quality but at a much lower cost. Herein lay Alvin's true genius and the foundation of his amazing success in becoming the largest clothing manufacturer in North America.

Hillel Becker, former president of Rubenstein Brothers
(equipment suppliers to the garment industry)

MY PEERLESS STORY

1

A Life Well Stitched

No one is more surprised than I am by the events that have taken place during my eighty-three years of life. The fact that I am able to write this story is almost unbelievable, but for me very exciting. Some people call me an "entrepreneur," but I don't really know what being an entrepreneur is. Yes, I operate a business, and I have taken financial risks to do so. However, I have never considered my actions too risky. All I've ever wanted to do was keep my job and move forward. That's always been my focus: keep the company going and take advantage of any opportunity. Even when things didn't go as planned or when I was faced with very hard decisions, I've always found a way to turn a negative into a positive and a threat into an opportunity. I am not an eternal optimist, but I do believe things will work out, somehow.

I was born in Albany, New York, on 19 September 1933. My mother, Betty Pearson Cramer, and my father, George Cramer, lived in the nearby town of Amsterdam, situated on the banks of the Mohawk River – the same town that produced Kirk Douglas, the Hollywood actor.

My mother's family lived in Albany, about a thirty-mile drive from Amsterdam, and I was born there at the Brady Maternity Hospital because my mother wanted to be close to her mother during the birth of her first child. When she met my father my mother was twenty-eight and working in the office of Van Heusen and Charles, a crystal and china shop in Albany. My father was six years older than her, handsome, popular, and actively involved

---

>>> Alvin Segal 4/8/2009 2:25 PM >>>

Dear Rabbi Wolpe,

First of all Hag Sameach, Have a sweet and happy Passover.

My name is Alvin Cramer Segal, and I read your article in JMag about Kirk Douglas.
I was born in Amsterdam, NY in 1933 as Alvin Cramer. My father passed away when I was 7
years old in 1940 when the war broke out. In 1948 my mother re-married Moe Segal and we
moved to Montreal, Canada - and I changed my name to Alvin Cramer Segal.

My mother always told me that Kirk Douglas worked as a young man for my late father George
Cramer, and his brother Sam Cramer at the S&G Cramer Co. on Main Street in Amsterdam, NY.

I have been very fortunate in my life to be a successful business man and philanthropist, and
certainly I share all of Kirk Douglas's reflections on Judaism and Philanthropy.

Could you find out if Kirk can verify any of his early days working for my father, or any stories he
may have of his life in Amsterdam.

I would love to hear of some stories about this period of time.

Thank you, Hag Sameach again

Alvin C. Segal

1.1a I tried to reach out to Kirk Douglas by way of an email to his rabbi.

in both Jewish and non-Jewish community organizations. They
married in October 1932 after a brief courtship and travelled to
New York City to board the ss *Southern Cross* for their honeymoon in Bermuda.

My father and his brother, Sam, were partners in a wholesale
grocery business called S and G Cramer Co. They also owned
a chain of retail grocery stores in the Albany/Amsterdam area.
My father was the inside man; he was the driving force behind
the business. Sam, who was an equal partner, handled sales.
The company was ahead of its time. During the years before the
Second World War it ran seven large supermarkets, unlike the
more common "mom and pop" stores.

The day after I was born, as my father drove home from the
hospital, his car veered off the road on the outskirts of Amsterdam.
He sustained serious injuries in the accident, most critically to his
back, and went from one surgery to the next for a good part of my

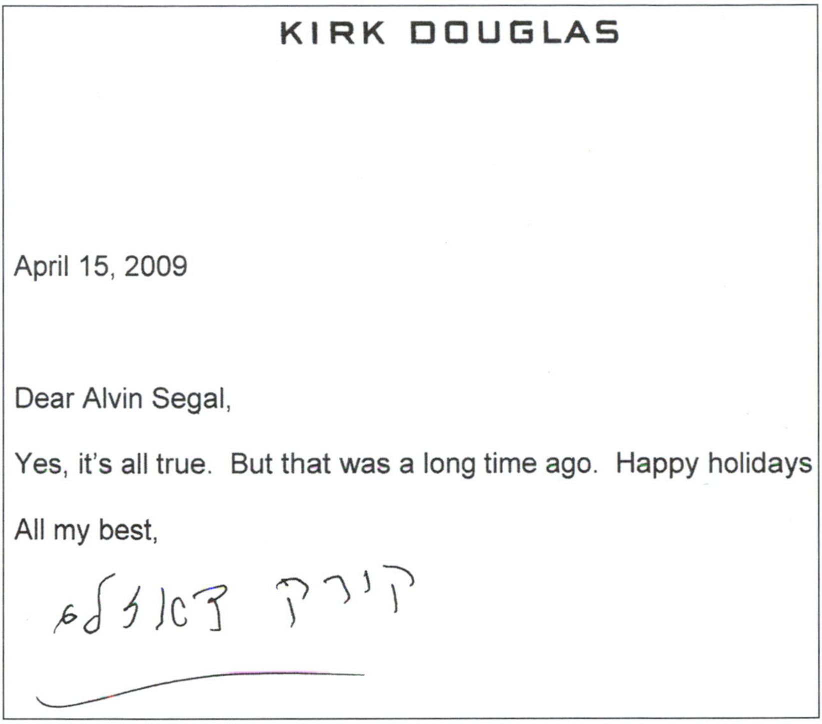

KIRK DOUGLAS

April 15, 2009

Dear Alvin Segal,

Yes, it's all true. But that was a long time ago. Happy holidays

All my best,

[handwritten signature in Hebrew-style script]

1.1b I ended up getting a response.

early childhood. To this day, the only memory I have of him being well was the time we spent at a local high-school baseball game. Unfortunately, I cannot recall any details from that day because I was so young. I only know that he was out of bed for a brief period of time.

Apparently, my parents' intimate relationship didn't suffer after the accident because my sister Connie was born two and a half years after me, and my younger sister Harriet a year after that.

Life was hard for my parents during those years. Though my father continued to work, he never fully regained his health and was mostly bedridden for the rest of his life, and his illness preoccupied the family and coloured most of my childhood memories. A cancerous tumour was discovered during one of his back surgeries. It was the middle of the Depression, they were raising three young children and maintaining a demanding business while coping with my father's chronic, ultimately fatal, illness.

1.2 My parents, George and Betty Cramer, boarding the
s s *Southern Cross* for their honeymoon, 1932.

1.3 My sisters and me, circa 1943: Harriet (six years old), Connie (eight), and me (ten).

Both my parents came from large families – my mother was one of nine children and my father of seven – and, as a result, we had a loving extended family of aunts, uncles, and cousins. On Sundays, especially, the Pearsons and Cramers would often gather at our home in Amsterdam, and there was always a sense of affection and good-natured teasing. Looking back, I think that with everything else going on, my mother and father went out of their way to make sure we felt connected to family.

I was named Alvin after my father's father, Abraham Cramer. Abraham had owned a shoemaking shop in Krustpils, a small *shtetl* in Latvia. In the spring of 1907 he, his wife Bessie, and six of their children sailed from Libau, Russia to America to escape the pogroms of Nicholas II. At Ellis Island the family's last name, Krumer, was changed to Cramer, and my father, who was nine at the time, went from Getzel to George. They settled in Schenectady, New York, where their eldest son, Mayer, who had sponsored them, was already making a life for himself. My mother's parents, Simon Pearson and Rose Phillips (originally Rakovsky, but changed by her brother Maier), were also from Russia, though my mother was born in Albany, New York.

From my earliest memories, being Jewish was a major part of my identity, mainly because my parents were observant of Jewish traditions and values. While my father was not *Shomer Shabbat* (a person who observes the Sabbath), on holidays like Rosh Hashanah and Yom Kippur we walked to synagogue. While he was alive, I wore *tzitzits* – knotted ritual fringes that remind Jews of their religious obligations – under my shirt.

My father was very involved in his synagogue, and this was commemorated by a marble plaque marking its fiftieth anniversary and rededication. The plaque was over the water fountain, and as a young child of five and six, every time I took a drink there the sight of my father's name filled me with pride. Years later, when the synagogue moved to a new location, I managed to acquire the plaque. It remains in my office at Peerless as a souvenir of my past and in memory of the father I never really knew.

I was very close to my mother and helped her around the house whenever I could – cleaning, running errands, and, most of all, fixing anything that was broken. From an early age, I was fascinated by all things mechanical – toys, appliances, and tools. I had a great knack for taking things apart, figuring out what made them work, and putting them back together. I think that's why I've always felt more at home on a factory floor than sitting in the front office. I like to see how things work.

The summer before I turned seven, I was sent to Camp Walden on Trout Lake, near Lake George in the Adirondack Mountains, about two hours from home. I bawled my eyes out and my mother

1.4 The synagogue rededication plaque honouring my father, George Cramer, 1937.

cried too. I now realize that she probably wanted me out of the house because my father's condition was worsening. When I returned from camp I started grade two, and just a few weeks after my seventh birthday my father called me into his room. "Alvin, I'm going away on a long trip," he said, "and from now on you'll be the man of the house. You have to look after your mother and sisters." I didn't understand what he was telling me or why. I listened to what he said, then went back outside to play. He passed away the next day, 26 October 1940, only three weeks after his forty-second birthday.

I didn't know what dying meant. All I remember is that he wasn't there anymore, and for many years after that day I was afraid of being in the dark.

My sisters and I didn't go to my father's funeral, perhaps because our mother felt that we were too young and would be traumatized. It may have been the right decision since my cousin Barbara remembers the terrible sound of my grandmother's inconsolable sobbing when they buried my father. My father was buried in the Free Jewish Cemetery (now called Agudat Achim cemetery) in Schenectady, the town where he grew up, about fifteen miles from Amsterdam. He was the first of my grandparents' grown children to pass away.

After my father died, my mother stayed in Amsterdam, with both sides of the family visiting us every weekend. I became very conscious of the value of family relationships and those connections have remained an important part of my life. My mother continued to keep a kosher home, and we observed all the Jewish holidays. Every Friday night my mother would light candles for the Shabbat, which lasts from sunset on Friday until Saturday after dusk. She always gave me the feeling that it was a very special day. No work is permitted during the Shabbat, so I wasn't allowed to write or cut paper. On Passover, we used Passover dishes and cutlery and made sure the house was kept kosher. She instilled in me the importance of tradition, and inspired my lifelong search for what it means to be Jewish.

Two years after my father's passing, my mother sold our house in Amsterdam, located at 17 Pershing Road, and rented a house in Albany, at 35 Manning Boulevard, to be closer to her family. As a widow with three small children, she needed all the support she could get. Knowing he was very ill, my father had bought an insurance policy that, in the event of his death, would pay my mother $150 a month for the rest of her life. At the time, it seemed like a small fortune. S and G Cramer Co. had an insurance policy that covered the cost of buying out a deceased partner's shares should one of the partners pass away. So we had that money as well and felt provided for. I remember that we also had a family car, a black De Soto, that I carefully washed on a regular basis.

My uncle Sam had a difficult time getting by in the business after my father died, and the hardships and shortages that came during the Second World War only made matters worse. After a few years, S and G Cramer Co. was reorganized and my uncle was left with only one retail grocery store.

I was glad to leave Amsterdam after my father died. On Sundays and holidays in Albany, we would all go to my grandmother Rose Pearson's house at 246 Morris Street. My mother's sister Sadie and her husband Bill Slawsky lived upstairs with their two children,

Hilly and Leo. My sisters and I would spend hours playing with all our cousins, and I remember those as happy, exciting gatherings with plenty of good food and laughter. My cousin Hilly was my babysitter, and we became very close. She helped my mother whenever she could. Hilly now lives in Honolulu and, as I write this, has turned ninety years old. In the fall of 2016, I made a trip to Hawaii to visit Hilly and her family. Today, more than seventy-five years after my father's death and our move to Albany, we still hold a Pearson family reunion every five years. Last year we celebrated our reunion in Stowe, Vermont, with more than fifty family members attending; some were young second and third cousins I met for the first time.

Our lives, like the lives of all Americans, changed when the country entered the Second World War. All of a sudden, every grownup conversation was about the war in Europe, about Hitler, and about Japan. People were concerned about what was happening, though at that time nobody realized the full extent of what the Jewish people in Poland and Germany were facing. There was a constant buzz of tension in the air and a strong sense of collective, energetic patriotism. In Albany, the capital of New York State, there was a feeling that big decisions were being made nearby, and I felt especially close to the centre of decision-making since the mayor of Albany, Erastus Corning II, lived up the street from my grandmother. On Saturdays we would go to the movie theatre, and the newsreels would blare headlines about the latest great victories by the allied forces. In those days before the twenty-four-hour news cycle, the news you saw at the movies on Saturday was still news, even if it was a week old. Everything related to the war; every newspaper headline and radio news report emphasized the war and what we could or couldn't do or have because of our engagement in the conflict.

My heroes weren't baseball players or movie stars. They were Franklin Roosevelt, General Dwight Eisenhower, and General Douglas MacArthur. F.D.R.'s "Fireside Chats" brought the whole neighbourhood to a standstill as people gathered around their radios; Eisenhower was fighting the Nazis in Europe and MacArthur was waging battle after battle in the South Pacific. We all idolized them – kids and grownups alike. They were like gods to us.

All everyone talked about was the war effort. My older cousin Leo and my Uncle George Pearson enlisted – it was the patriotic thing to do. None of my family died in the war but neighbours were killed in Europe and in the Philippines. Leo was awarded three purple hearts. Every day in school we pledged allegiance to the flag. The war wasn't talked about just in terms of military victories; it was seen as a battle between conflicting values: of good versus evil. It was potent stuff for a little boy, and I'll never forget the celebrations when battles were won.

As the war dragged on, my mother began to worry. Not only were everyday staples like sugar, soap, meat, and gasoline rationed, but also inflation was taking a sizeable bite out of our monthly $150. She never complained or showed her concern to my sisters or me; she just made a greater effort to do more with less. She had gone from being a comfortable widow in the years before the war to struggling to maintain that illusion for herself and for us. Meanwhile, I did what I could to make life easier for her by fixing things around the house that we couldn't afford to replace. We also spent a lot of time at my grandmother's, and I always enjoyed following my Uncle Bill Slawsky around his house upstairs. He showed me how to use tools and fix things.

I remember being a skinny, generally happy kid, riding my bike around town, teasing my sisters Connie and Harriet, and struggling with my schoolwork. I had what would probably now be diagnosed as attention deficit disorder or some other learning disability, and school wasn't easy for me, especially English class because my spelling was atrocious. I also had a terrible stutter, which affected everything from my school performance to my social interactions. It was so bad that I wasn't allowed to answer the phone, because I couldn't get "Hello" out fast enough.

My sister Connie remembers me as a hyperactive kid. "I have a vision of him as a kid and you just couldn't catch him. My mother would be running after him around the dining-room table and he'd be out the door. But he was having a good time – there was nothing malicious about him. She couldn't control him. He wasn't bad, you just couldn't nail him down."

When I left Arnold Avenue School in Amsterdam and started grade three at School No. 16 in Albany, I had to adjust to being the new kid, fatherless, and with a stutter to boot. I failed grades three, four, and five, so it must have had an impact on me. I never repeated a year though because they kept moving me ahead "on trial." One day, my mother told me we had to go talk to the principal. When we got to his office, he said, "Alvin, do you want to be the dumbest kid in grade five or the smartest kid in grade four?" I answered, "The dumbest kid in grade five." So that was that. That was my character then and still is to this day; I always move forward and let people think I don't know what's going on. Maybe I like people underestimating me; it gives me time to come up with an answer that will surprise them.

During the Second World War, no one in the United States knew what was happening to the Jews in Europe, and anti-Semitism on the home front was rampant. Some kids in my class probably had no idea what they were saying or doing, but it seemed that non-Jewish kids took every chance they got to tease us. I had a fight almost every day walking from our house on Manning Boulevard to School No. 16 because of anti-Semitic bullies.

I never talked to my mother about the fights, but it was a good thing I was small – like the ninety-seven-pound weakling in the Charles Atlas ads in comic books – and fast because I was able to outrun just about anyone. I never really understood why they treated us differently. I was too young to process anti-Semitism as a phenomenon, and my mother never talked about it. It was just part of our lives.

After school I would ride my bicycle to Hebrew school, about two miles from home, and that long bike ride to the Ohav Shalom Synagogue on Western Avenue was the best part of my day. Hebrew school was even more problematic than regular school, since reading the Hebrew alphabet was almost impossible. After three years (and until my Bar Mitzvah) I never progressed beyond grade one. When I had children, I chose to send all three to a Jewish parochial day school, "The Jewish People's School," in Montreal. I'm enormously proud of that decision; it's something I never experienced myself. They became somewhat fluent in the Hebrew language and developed a strong affiliation with Israel and being Jewish.

We couldn't afford to travel much in those days, so when my mother surprised me with train tickets to attend my cousin Allan Strean's Bar Mitzvah in Ottawa, Ontario, I was very excited. I was nine years old, had never been outside of the Albany area, and had no idea where Canada was, so it seemed like a wonderful adventure. We rode the train to Montreal, stayed overnight at my mother's cousin Bessie Segal's home, and the next day travelled to Ottawa for the ceremony and celebration.

My mother was happy to spend a night in Montreal with Bessie, one of her favourite cousins from the Montreal branch of the Pearson family. Bessie had two sisters living in Montreal, Ethel and Tessa. My mother made sure to stay in touch with all three and would talk to them whenever she could. Bessie was married to a well-liked gentleman named Moe Segal. They had two teenage daughters, Rya and Greta. Moe was fifty-per-cent owner of a men's suit manufacturing company called Peerless. He would later become my stepfather, and Peerless would become my company. But on that long-ago night of our big trip, he was just the husband of my mother's cousin, and I don't remember anything about him from that visit.

When I was eleven, I found out that I would be shipped off to boarding school for grades seven and eight. I had apparently failed grade six and the only way to advance to grade seven was to go to a private boarding school. I don't know how my mother came up with the money but I guess she felt she didn't have a choice. By that time, and by all accounts, I had become too much for her to handle – she was coping with raising three young children without a husband and on limited resources. To this day, both my sisters insist that I used to tease them, so I guess I probably did. I felt like a regular kid except for one thing: my stutter, which wasn't getting any better.

There was nothing I wanted less than to go off to Tarrytown, New York, to live at the Irving Prep School for Boys. I was doubly shocked to learn I'd only be allowed to come home for the holidays. All my crying and arguing didn't change my mother's mind, and off I went to a massive Victorian-style building that squatted on a hill overlooking the Hudson River.

My mother put me on the train in Albany for the two-hour ride to Poughkeepsie, New York. The train was pulled by a steam engine, which was switched to an electric engine in Poughkeepsie for the onward trip to Tarrytown and eventually to New York City. In those days, steam engines were not allowed within twenty-five miles of New York City. The most exciting part of the trip was standing on the platform watching the engines change. I loved the way the steam engine was released and the electric engine became coupled to the train. For a kid who loved to take things apart and fix them, it was fascinating.

The Irving Prep School for Boys was named after Washington Irving, author of *The Legend of Sleepy Hollow*, and was in North Tarrytown. The best thing about Irving was the amazing view of the river from my bedroom window. It was 1944–45 and I remember looking out and seeing fleets of warships lined up on the Hudson River. The routine and discipline at Irving had an influence on me; I did much better academically during those two years. That period affected my attitude and outlook on life. Somehow, it made me feel more responsible for myself. They didn't teach me how to spell any better, but my roommate, Peter Wodtke, with whom I'm still in touch, was the smartest kid in the class, and he helped me with English. It seemed like every kid in our class was from some sort of broken home with either divorced or widowed parents, so I didn't feel like such an outsider. My best memory from Irving was the day we all went into New York City by bus to see a Yankees baseball game. I still love the Yankees because of the excitement of that day.

My Bar Mitzvah was planned for 17 August 1946 (*Parsha Ekev*) at congregation Ohav Sholom in Albany. At the end of my second year at Irving I was sent to a speech therapy camp in Providence, Rhode Island, with the hope that I'd be cured of my stutter for the big event. (On the bus ride to camp, the FBI stopped us because they thought there was a spy on the bus. It was the summer of 1946; the war was over but there was still a lot of tension in the air.) I spent eight weeks at camp going through breathing and enunciation lessons and learning sign language for backup. When I arrived home in Albany at the end of the summer, everyone was thrilled that my stutter was gone. But when I woke up the next morning, there was the stutter again. I was devastated and felt terrible for my mother.

My stutter made me self-conscious and nervous about almost everything. It obviously weighed on my mother as well, because otherwise she wouldn't have spent money we didn't have to help me get rid of it. At the age of fifty-five, I needed dental surgery because of an abscess in my gum. During the surgery, the nerves in my upper gums were severed, and it was this unusual "lucky run-in" with the surgeon that actually made my stutter disappear. Someone should patent that procedure as a cure for stutterers. But back in Albany, at almost thirteen years old (the rabbi said that because I didn't have a father I had to become a man earlier), I still stuttered, and I still had to make my Bar Mitzvah speech.

The big day arrived, the synagogue was full, and it was harder than ever for me to get the words out. The speech was a short one, but no speech is short for a stutterer. I tried every trick I'd learned at speech camp, but I was so nervous that I couldn't even look at the rabbi when he addressed me. Somehow, eventually, I managed to say: "Worthy rabbi, beloved mother, and dear friends: today, I am a man."

My sister Connie remembers the tension from that event. "Alvin's a wonderful example of people who are born different and find ways to succeed despite their disabilities," she said recently. "His stutter didn't seem to hold him back. He just kept going and doing his thing. It bothered him, there's no question. At his Bar Mitzvah, he had to come up and face an audience and he just did it. It was probably a tremendous amount of pressure." Connie added, "My mother would never believe it if she saw how he's turned out."

After two years at Irving I didn't have to return, probably because my mother could no longer afford it. I didn't care what the reason was, I was just happy to be starting grade nine at Hackett Junior High in Albany. A year had passed since the war ended, and inflation had devalued my mother's income. The monthly $150 we had lived on was then worth about $100, and we had moved from Manning Boulevard into a tiny, dilapidated house on New Scotland Avenue. Times were tough for everyone, and they seemed especially tough for us. My mother would pinch pennies to make ends meet. We weren't allowed to waste a bite of food or leave a room without turning off the light. I didn't know the dire straits we were in until later, after our lives had changed for the better.

Only once the war was over did we begin to hear stories of what had happened to the Jewish people of Europe. (How could we have not known what was happening in Poland and Germany? Nothing like that could happen today without the world knowing about it.) The shock of the concentration camps, the photographs and stories of the survivors started making headlines around the world. The idea of forming the State of Israel came alive with Jewish people worldwide talking about the Holocaust and about having their own country. The Zionist dream of a Jewish homeland finally seemed like a real possibility. It was in the newspapers, on the radio, and was part of every discussion, and I was very aware of it.

The conversation built for three years, and then came the momentous event. I have a vivid memory of standing beside the radio with my mother and listening as the United Nations voted on the creation of the State of Israel. The decision was made official on 14 May 1948. We were filled with joy. There was still anti-Semitism, but now the Jewish people had a country of their own. Although I was a young boy when the war ended, those years made an impression on me that has lasted my whole life, and triggered my interest in the history of the Jewish people. The creation of the State of Israel under such difficult circumstances played a distinct role in my future, and from that moment on, my dream was to visit Israel.

One day, my mother received a letter postmarked "Montreal." It was an invitation to the wedding of Greta Segal, Moe and the late Bessie's youngest daughter. My mother was happy to accept but also saddened, because the last time she had been in Montreal was for cousin Bessie's funeral, two years earlier. Like my father, Bessie passed away from cancer at a young age.

What I found out years later was that the invitation came with an ulterior motive. Moe Segal was lonely after Bessie's death and it had occurred to Bessie's sisters, Ethel and Tessa, that my mother might be a good match for him. Moe's sisters-in-law were very persuasive and they probably influenced Moe to welcome my mother to Montreal by saying, "Hello Betty, let's get married!" It turned out they were right, because when she returned home from the wedding, my mother announced her engagement. As soon as the school year ended, we would be moving to Montreal.

This news didn't upset me. I was happy to leave Albany, maybe because I was struggling to get through grade nine or because things had become so hard for us. Life was clearly not easy for my mother, who was on her own with three children and down to her last penny. I must have thought that living anywhere would be better than our shack on New Scotland Avenue.

Moe Segal came to Albany in the early spring of 1948, and he and my mother were married in a small ceremony. My mother told him she wanted to remain in Albany until our school year ended in June, so after the wedding Moe returned to Montreal on his own. Even then, I thought it was courageous of Moe to marry a woman with three young children, and I've often wondered if he knew what he was getting into and how it would affect all our lives.

As the school year drew to a close, we packed our belongings into suitcases and boxes, the car was stuffed with our most prized possessions, and early on the morning of 25 June 1948 I squeezed into the back seat for the long drive to Montreal. I was happy. I was fourteen years old, and my main thought was that I had passed all my subjects in school, especially mathematics, which I was good at. I had completed grade nine and was looking forward to a new summer camp. My mother drove with her sister, my aunt Celia, settled in next to her. My sisters had left by train two days earlier. In those days, it took a whole day to drive from Albany to Montreal because there was no interstate highway. We headed up on Route 9 north, which took us to the border crossing at Lacolle, Quebec. I had only been to Canada once and could never have imagined what was to come.

When we arrived at customs, we told them we were moving to Canada and, after an hour of filling out forms, were declared landed immigrants (a similar status to that conferred by a US green card). That's how it worked in those days. When I arrived in Montreal later that day, I found out that when my sisters crossed the border, they had told the custom agents they were only visiting Canada. Two years later, on a return trip from Europe, both my sisters became landed immigrants like me.

My greatest memory of arriving in Montreal was the sight of the streetcars. I had never seen anything like them, with their fixed rails and overhead wires and, being mechanically inclined, I was transfixed. The number sixty-five went up Côte-des-Neiges Road, past the Shelbourne Towers at 3787 Côte-des-Neiges, the four-storey red brick building where Moe had been living in a two-bedroom apartment since he'd been widowed. It was our first address in Montreal, though my sisters and I never had a chance to live there.

Two days after we arrived in Montreal, my sisters and I were sent off to Camp Winnebago, where we would spend our next few summers. After camp, when we got back to Montreal, I returned to my cot in the den at the Shelbourne Towers. I slept there only a few nights, since soon we were off to our next destination, a boarding school, Stanstead College, in Quebec's Eastern Townships near the Vermont border.

My sisters, Connie and Harriet, and I were always together. The three of us were as close as a brother and two sisters could be, especially given all we had been through from my father's death to my mother's remarriage. They both grew up to be remarkable women and great mothers, each with four children. Harriet and her husband Jack Lazare live in Montreal and have six grandchildren, and Connie made *aliyah* to Israel with her husband Chuck Solomon and their four young children. Connie lives there to this day surrounded by her children, twenty-four grandchildren, and six great-grandchildren and counting.

When we were at Stanstead, my sister's friends became my friends, and being Connie's big brother was an excellent way to meet girls. That's how I met my first girlfriend. Her name was Dorothy and she was Connie's roommate at Stanstead. To me, a kid with a stutter who struggled academically and had to muster his gumption from sources that are still a mystery, having a girlfriend seemed like a miracle.

1.5 Moe Segal and my mother, Betty, happy newlyweds, late 1940s.

All in all, I had a great time during my two years at Stanstead. Academically, they were easier than my previous school years because I started in grade nine, which I had finished the year before in Albany. My sisters and I had to repeat the year we'd already completed because in Quebec high school finished after grade eleven, not twelve. Despite my stutter, I had one line in Thornton Wilder's play *Our Town*, three words, "Morning, Doc Gibbs," and managed to get it out just fine. While I hadn't been a star athlete in Albany – couldn't make water boy – my basic basketball and football skills made me a hero on both the court and the field in Canada, the land of hockey. In sports, my nickname was "American." I got into great physical shape at Stanstead because the football training was so rigorous. During my second summer at Camp Winnebago I was in such good physical shape, I became the best athlete at camp.

Every week the whole school was obliged to attend church; all the students would get decked out in our Sunday best and walk across the street to the United Church in the town of Stanstead. Even at church the boys found ways to get into trouble. Some of my classmates were experts at slipping one quarter into the collection plate and palming two back. As one of the few Jewish students in the school, I wasn't too bothered by the church service because there weren't big crosses everywhere. I got through by crossing my fingers and singing under my breath, "Onward *Jewish* soldiers, marching unto war, with the *Star of David*." Even though the war had ended and Israel had been declared a country, anti-Semitism persisted. I got into one fight that was so bad I almost lost a tooth. A classmate called me a "dirty Jew" so I jumped on him, pushed him to the ground, and sat on top of him. His fists were flying and before I could pin him down, one connected with my mouth.

During the summer of 1950, Moe Segal and his younger brother, Hy, bought a duplex at 4900–4902 Isabella Ave, on the corner of Lemieux Street in a newly developed neighbourhood called "Snowdon." My sisters and I had returned from camp at the end of August and discovered that our mother and Moe had already moved in. We liked the new house and the neighbourhood a lot. Today Snowdon is considered very central and is a melting pot of ethnic groups speaking languages ranging from Arabic to Zulu, but back then it was a Jewish neighbourhood. There was no Hampstead or Côte-St-Luc yet – it seemed like all the Jewish people of Montreal lived in Snowdon.

Our new home was the seven-room bottom-half of a duplex. Connie and Harriet shared a bedroom on the main floor, and I had my own bedroom in the basement. Hy lived with his wife, Avie, and son, Melvin, upstairs. Our back doors were always open and I spent a lot of time upstairs, mostly babysitting Melvin. Moe's other brother, Phil, and his family lived around the corner on Jean-Brillant. Snowdon felt like one big family, not just because Moe's family lived nearby but also because I felt like I finally had a secure home. Our mother was happy, and so were we. My sisters and I became friendly with our neighbours in the Snowdon area and we still keep in touch with many of them today.

After passing grades nine and ten at Stanstead, I entered grade eleven (the last year of high school) at Montreal High School on University Avenue. My most difficult subject was French, which had been much easier at an English boarding school where the concentration on French was much less than at a public Montreal high school. To supplement my classes at high school, I went to a private French tutor four days a week. During that year, my sisters and I became closer than ever. Unlike the kids born in Montreal, I had no friends other than my classmates, and, with Moe and my mother travelling and away from home most of the time, my sisters and I had to stick together. There were only four other Jewish kids in my grade, but I don't remember encountering any anti-Semitism at Montreal High or getting into any fistfights. I did make new friends among my schoolmates though, some of whom I'm still friends with to this day.

By that time, I had learned to be self-reliant, to start over again and again in new environments with new challenges. I had to learn in unconventional ways because the conventional ones didn't work for me. Most of all, I learned to adapt; it was what I had become very good at.

The year my sisters and I started at Montreal High, my mother told Connie and Harriet to change their last names to Segal. They were starting out at a new school, in a new city, and it was the right time to make that change. I remember my mother saying that when women got married they took their husband's name, so Connie and Harriet wouldn't keep the Cramer name anyway. It was an easy decision for them. I wasn't sure why then and I never really found out, but I kept the name Cramer. I was already self-conscious because of my stutter and now I had a different last name from my mother and sisters, so I wasn't too happy about it. Whenever someone asked me why my name was Cramer and not Segal, I'd have to go over the whole story, with my stutter. All I wanted was to be like every other teenager; I didn't want the attention.

I hadn't had much contact with Moe Segal up to that point because of camp and boarding school. Moe was my mother's husband but I knew nothing about him. We did not have a typical father-son relationship, and I found it difficult to call Moe "Dad" because we hardly ever had conversations. When I was in grade eleven and living at home, I finally started to get to know him a little better, and that's when I began calling him "Dad." I didn't have a clue what he did for a living, but I could tell he was smart and successful. Moe was sophisticated too, a guy who knew how to live in style; I remember there was a little silver bell on the dining room table that my mother rang to summon the housekeeper. Moe's company owned a thirty-five-foot yacht called the *Sea Gal*, which was kept at the Iroquois Yacht Club (now called the Lachine Yacht Club). Moe and my mother would invite different members of the family and friends for afternoons on the boat; it was a real treat to go swimming at the sand bar in Lake St-Louis.

The boat had a full-time captain named Mac, who would sail the *Sea Gal* down to Florida during the winter months. Moe was fifty when he and my mother married and already semiretired, which meant he finished his workday at lunchtime. They were still travelling a lot, including spending the winters in Florida, so my sisters and I were left alone with the housekeeper most of the time.

In June 1951, I wrote my final high-school exams and went off to Camp Winnebago, this time as a junior counsellor. The camp had one sailboat, and I was very happy and excited to take my campers on the boat when it was on their schedule of activities. I became hooked on sailing from that experience.

1.6 The *Sea Gal* yacht at the sandbar in Lac St Louis, 1952.

I was at camp having the time of my life when suddenly, one day in August, I was called in from outside for a phone call. It was my mother. She told me that I had failed French, which, in Quebec, meant that I couldn't graduate from high school. I had to leave camp immediately to go home and study for my supplemental French oral and written exams. A couple of weeks later, I received my new marks. They were worse than the results from my first exam; they had actually dropped from 23/200 to a total of 18/200.

When I found out that I had failed my second French exam and therefore wouldn't be graduating from high school, I broke down and cried. After all the tutoring and all the pressure, I couldn't believe my whole life was now derailed because of one subject. I had no way of knowing it was the crisis that would change my life.

The same night I received my test results, Moe called me into the den. I had no idea what to expect from the conversation I was

1.7 During the summer of 1951 I was a junior counsellor at Camp Winnebago. I'm seated at the stern of canoe #4.

about to have with him. He was a distant figure who impressed me, but I really knew nothing about him and he didn't know me any better. I was very nervous and my stuttering was even worse than usual, so much so that I could barely get out the word "Dad" when I entered the room. Moe was sitting comfortably in his chair when he said to me, "You're not much of a student, Alvin. You have a choice: you can go back to Albany where you came from and continue your schooling there, where the French won't matter, or I can give you a job in my factory for $35 a week." I was in shock! Moe and I hardly ever talked, and there he was, out of the blue, offering me a job.

In hindsight, I realize that offering me a job was the easiest way for Moe to make me responsible for myself and not his burden. But for me, it wasn't a tough choice. I didn't know exactly what Moe Segal did for a living – I'd never been in a factory and barely had a notion of what working full-time was like, but what I heard was "$35 a week." In those days that was a lot of money, and I'd have no more worries about school.

It was the day before my eighteenth birthday. We agreed I could wait an extra day and start working on 20 September 1951.

2

Life Begins at Eighteen: It's *Bashert*

On the day I started at Peerless, my mother suggested during breakfast, "Why don't you change your name to Segal?" She knew that having the last name Cramer, while Connie and Harriet were named Segal, bothered me. "Okay, how do you spell Segal?" I asked jokingly. I knew how to spell Segal even if I wasn't so great at spelling anything else. It was strange to think of going from being Alvin Cramer to Alvin Segal, but a fresh start is a fresh start. I put no thought or importance into the impact changing my name would have on me, and I didn't realise at that moment how my new name would affect my future either.

That morning, when I changed my last name, a new branch of the Segal family was born. There was no discussion about it with Moe or anyone else. Changing my name just made things a bit more comfortable for my mother, for Moe, and for me at Peerless. To me I was still Alvin Cramer but now known as Alvin Cramer Segal. I had no thought at that moment that the Segal name would be passed on to my children and grandchildren and, of course, had no idea that later it would be associated with some of the most important things in my life, including the Segal Comprehensive Cancer Centre at the Montreal Jewish General Hospital and the Segal Centre for the Performing Arts in Montreal. I legally changed my name to Alvin Cramer Segal several years later.

That morning, Moe drove me to work at the Peerless factory and office at 55 Pine Avenue East on the north-east corner of St Dominique. The company had a lease on the entire building, which

2.1 "Canada's Best Value in Clothing." The Peerless office and factory building at the corner of Pine and St Dominique, 1951.

was about 24,000 square feet over four floors. It was a red brick building with the Peerless logo embedded in the marble floor of its entrance (still there to this day), and on the roof was a big sign that read "Peerless Clothes. Canada's Best Value in Clothing."

When we arrived at the office, Moe introduced me to everyone as "My son, Alvin Segal." It was almost like a birth announcement in the newspaper: "Moe Segal announces the arrival of a son, Alvin. 160 lbs, 70 inches long." The question "Where did he come from?" was certainly on everybody's mind. Introducing me that way must have made an impression on everyone, since they knew that Moe didn't have a son.

Moe founded Peerless Clothing in 1919 and soon after took in his brother Phil as his partner. When I started working at Peerless, Moe and Phil were each fifty-per-cent owners, and members of their family were everywhere in the company except in the factory. Phil was at home recovering from a heart attack. His twenty-one-year-old son, Hershey Segal, had left his studies at McGill University to run the company with Moe. (It was obvious there was no one else in the family capable enough to help Moe manage Peerless.) Hershey's older brother, Ralph, worked in the shipping room. Moe's father worked in the cutting room part-time; his two brothers-in-law and his younger brother, Hy, ran a boys' suit division: P. Segal Co.; Moe's high-school friend, Harry Diamond, was the designer (he was really the pattern-maker, but back then we called them "designers") in charge of running the factory with his brother, George Diamond, who ran the cutting room. Moe's cousin, Jack Levitt, ran the shipping room and another cousin, Moe Smith, made the buttonholes in the jackets. Phil's brother-in-law, Martin Goldsmith, was the controller, and Moe and Phil's sister, Esther Lewis, worked in the office. Moe's best friend, Cecil Usher, was the company's auditor, and Moe's brother-in-law's brother, Harry Blanshay, was the company lawyer. It truly was a family business.

That morning, Moe called Harry Diamond from the factory upstairs into the office and said, "Harry, my son Alvin is going to be working with you in the factory; show him how it works and what's going on." There was no discussion between us about my job, Harry just put his arm around me and said, "I'll teach you in five years what it took me twenty-five to learn."

We walked upstairs to the factory and Harry put me at a table in the coat shop and gave me a job pairing-in collars (pairing the top collar with the felt under-collar). My job at Peerless truly did start with the collar. That same day Harry introduced me to Sam Kirsch, who was the head quality man, and his son, Benny, the coat shop foreman. Benny took me through the factory, to the coat shop, the pants shop, and the cutting room, and introduced me to all the foremen and key people.

For someone like me, obsessed with machines and systems and how pieces come together, the factory was fascinating. Men's suit manufacturing is about fitting one piece to another on an assembly line with all the noise, hustle, and bustle that that entails. When I started at Peerless, there were about 300 people working in the factory and cutting room. There were sewing machines and pressing machines, and foremen running every section where each worker at every station performed very specific and sometimes highly specialized tasks, from marker making to cutting to sewing pockets to sewing in sleeves, etc., that all contributed to the final product.

Moe hadn't given me an actual job and Harry hadn't said anything after assigning me to pairing collars, so the next day I returned to my table and kept doing the same thing. I figured I would eventually learn about the rest of the factory and what my job was to be. The factory was not considered an ideal place to work so none of the Segal family worked in it; they were all in the shipping room or the office. But I didn't mind. For me, it was heaven. I loved the factory from the minute I walked in. Little did I realize that Peerless was to become my *soul mate*.

I remember Moe's saying: "You learn by listening, not by talking!" and those words have stayed with me my whole life. I've always believed asking questions is the best way to learn. At Peerless, I was starting from zero, and in those first days and weeks I must have asked a million questions. I talked to the foremen and asked them "Why? Why? Why? What is this? What is that? Why do we do it this way?" I wanted to start learning and to help out right away, so I asked people what they were doing and if there was a way to make their jobs easier. Most people at Peerless were exceedingly friendly and helpful and loved talking about their work. I don't know whether they thought I was a pest they had to put up with because I was Moe Segal's son, but pretty soon they were telling me not just how things worked but why some things didn't work, which increased my learning curve. For a man of few words because of a stutter, I managed to get answers and learned as much as I could.

The motto of the company was "Canada's best value in clothing" and our product reflected that. In those days, all we made at Peerless were low-priced suits and odd trousers from synthetic rayon fabrics, and sport coats of woollen blends. ("Odd trousers" is the industry term for pants without matching suit-jackets). Woollen blends don't have the same properties as the worsted wool used in fine clothing, but are a good choice if you want to spend less money and still get some of the benefits of wool. They were inexpensive, affordable suits destined for what Moe Segal called the "lunch bucket" consumer and retailed for under twenty dollars and came with two pairs of pants, sometimes three. Most men in the country, even farmers, had at least one suit in their closet. Every man also had an overcoat, so we started making those too.

Moe was selling Peerless suits at the opening price point in specialty stores and to places like Eaton's basement (the discount section of Eaton's department store). You could buy a Peerless suit in a pawnshop on Craig Street, and we were selling all over Canada too. As well as its factory in Montreal, the company had leased a plant in Amherst, Nova Scotia, during the Second World War to manufacture uniforms. Peerless had a warehouse in Toronto and salesmen in western Canada, the Ottawa valley, and the Maritimes. The salesman covering the Maritimes was named Aaron Levine. Eventually, three generations of Levine's worked for Peerless: Aaron, his son Jack, and Jack's son Gary, who retired in 2016.

In the 1950s, Montreal was one of the major garment centers in North America and had a very big Jewish community. Before and especially after the war, a large number of Jewish immigrants came to Montreal, many of them skilled in the needle trade. At Peerless, about half the operators on the factory floor were French Canadian and the other half were Jewish, many of them Holocaust survivors. It was from the Jewish operators at Peerless that I learned so much about the Holocaust. So many of them were survivors who had lost family, and they shared their stories and photos with me.

The pain and loss caused by the war was still very present less than a decade after Hitler's defeat and the liberation of the concentration camps. One time I bought a sewing machine for the factory from West Germany – a Durkopp – because it was very efficient and would pay for itself in less than a year. Thirty days after the machine was up and running in the factory, the invoice came into the office. When Phil Segal saw it on his desk, he called me in and said, "We don't buy machines from West Germany – get it out of here!" I explained that it was saving us money because it was so efficient, but he was adamant. I had to stand outside on

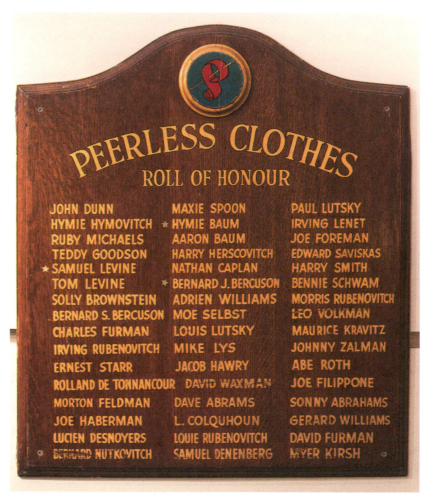

PEERLESS CLOTHES
ROLL OF HONOUR

JOHN DUNN	MAXIE SPOON	PAUL LUTSKY
HYMIE HYMOVITCH	★ HYMIE BAUM	IRVING LENET
RUBY MICHAELS	AARON BAUM	JOE FOREMAN
TEDDY GOODSON	HARRY HERSCOVITCH	EDWARD SAVISKAS
★ SAMUEL LEVINE	NATHAN CAPLAN	HARRY SMITH
TOM LEVINE	★ BERNARD J. BERCUSON	BENNIE SCHWAM
SOLLY BROWNSTEIN	ADRIEN WILLIAMS	MORRIS RUBENOVITCH
BERNARD S. BERCUSON	MOE SELBST	LEO VOLKMAN
CHARLES FURMAN	LOUIS LUTSKY	MAURICE KRAVITZ
IRVING RUBENOVITCH	MIKE LYS	JOHNNY ZALMAN
ERNEST STARR	JACOB HAWRY	ABE ROTH
ROLLAND DE TONNANCOUR	DAVID WAXMAN	JOE FILIPPONE
MORTON FELDMAN	DAVE ABRAMS	SONNY ABRAHAMS
JOE HABERMAN	L. COLQUHOUN	GERARD WILLIAMS
LUCIEN DESNOYERS	LOUIE RUBENOVITCH	DAVID FURMAN
BERNARD NUTKOVITCH	SAMUEL DENENBERG	MYER KIRSH

2.2 Moe had a plaque made naming all Peerless employees who fought in the Second World War. Those with stars beside their names were killed in action. Today this plaque hangs in the lobby of our Pie-IX factory building.

the street in the rain until a truck came to pick the machine up. In those years, and for many years to follow, that's how negative feelings were about anything produced in Germany.

Although it was very hard work, the atmosphere in the factory was always friendly; people generally got along and it was like a big happy family. At that time, Peerless was one of the few men's suit manufacturers that wasn't in the sectoral union of the Amalgamated Clothing Workers of America (ACWA). Instead, we had what we called "the Peerless Club." The factory was closed for Jewish holidays and, after five years of service, all our employees (regardless of religion) were paid for those days. As well, there was no work on Saturdays – the Sabbath. These were benefits that didn't exist in the sectoral union factories and our employees appreciated that.

People were happy and had a lot of respect for Moe and Phil Segal. Phil was vice-president and in charge of administration, and Moe was the president and a phenomenal salesman. I was once standing near Moe when he was dealing with a picky customer. There were two rows of suits hanging back to back. The customer wasn't happy with the first suit Moe showed him. "Oh," Moe said, "I know exactly what you want." He went around to the other row of identical suits and brought one of them to the customer, who then agreed that it was the one he wanted.

As businessmen, Moe and Phil were well-respected, ethical people. During the war, they'd received an order from the Canadian Department of Munitions and Supply for military uniforms – "summer battle dress." After the order was filled, they sent a cheque back to the government for $4,737 covering not only the profit they had made on the contract but also their share of salaries during that time. In their accompanying letter to the department, they wrote: "We do not desire to receive any benefit or gain from this war contract." The finance minister, J.H. Ilsley, wrote back, "I am deeply touched by your cooperative and patriotic attitude." He noted that Peerless had "saved the government a substantial sum on the contract by bettering the contract price by seven cents a garment." Moe and Phil were noted in *Canada's Who's Who* at the time for that gesture.

After two months on the factory floor, I still did not have a job description or a punch card. Every morning I would just pick up wherever I'd left off the day before. I became very friendly with Paul Verchère, the mechanic who fixed all the sewing machines. My mother had a sewing machine at home, but the Peerless factory was full of noisy industrial machines and I'd certainly never taken one of those apart. I'd help him with repairs, which taught me even more about how the factory worked and where the problems were. In the early days, the tools we had to work with included a vice that was half broken. One day, I took a sledge-hammer and broke it completely to get it replaced.

Back then, we would call in outside servicemen for any repairs Paul couldn't handle, including plumbing, welding, and electrical work. My strength has always been fixing things, and slowly, over many years I've worked to have repairs all done in-house. Today we have a fully-equipped machine shop that not only handles repairs but also builds all kinds of modifications for the sewing operators.

Harry Diamond rarely ventured beyond his spot at the designing table, located at the end of the floor, and I didn't learn much from him because he left me pretty much to myself from the first day. Since my table was right beside the operators sewing on the collars, they told me that the collars didn't fit properly. When I went to Harry to see if we could fix them, he said, "Oh, I know the collars don't fit. I'll just add a little bit of fabric to them. The new pattern will be on the factory floor in four months." That's how long it took in those days, for a pattern change to hit the factory floor. Four months later, the collars still didn't fit because he'd added too much fabric. These were the kinds of frustrations I was learning about. (Today, with the advent of computers, we can change a pattern and everything is fixed right away.)

Collars became an early obsession of mine. If the collar doesn't hug the neck properly, the finished coat doesn't fit the way it should. In those days, the collar was the last part sewn onto the coat and it had to be altered by hand to fit properly. This caused delays in our production, a problem that led me, twenty-five years later, to introduce the engineered suit – a European innovation that made Peerless a global leader in its field. (More about that later.)

I still lived at home on 4900 Isabella Avenue, and at lunch and dinner I would talk with Moe, asking questions and telling him what was going on in the factory. "Today, I did button holes."

"Today, I did sleeves." I would tell him about an improvement we had made or a way we could reduce or "save" an operator for improved efficiency and costs. He just listened to me and retained everything. He probably discovered more about his factory than he had in years by listening to me every night. He must have liked what he heard, because he gave me a free hand, didn't question my suggestions, and whenever I had an idea, he would tell me, "Try it. If it doesn't work, you'll fix it."

Harry and I got along in the early days, but the more I learned about the factory, talking to the foremen and operators, the less I had to do with him. At Christmas time the first year, I was told that there was a collection taking place for Harry's annual gift. The foremen each had to give ten dollars, and someone asked me to donate. That night at dinner, I asked Moe, very innocently, if I had to contribute ten dollars for a gift for Harry Diamond. I don't know whether Moe had known about this tradition, but he said I didn't have to contribute. The next day, I went back to the man who'd asked me to contribute and told him Moe had told me I didn't have to give. The collection stopped that day, and I never knew why.

By the time I started at Peerless, Moe never set foot in the factory, and I became his link to what was going on there. Until then, Moe heard of changes only from Harry Diamond. Moe would sometimes joke around and say that if Harry had "saved" all the employees he claimed he had, by making their operations more efficient, there'd have been no one left working in the factory.

Since Moe was semiretired and didn't return to work after lunch, I'd drive back to Peerless with Ralph, Phil's son, who lived on the next street. Ralph and I became quite friendly. He was very easy to get along with and I enjoyed the drive back to work with him. Ralph was four years older than I and looked a lot like his father, Phil. We would talk about what was going on in the company and about the Segal family. I got to know an awful lot about all the cousins and distant family members. Getting closer to Moe and Ralph made me feel as though I was part of the Segal family.

When I was almost nineteen, my mother wanted to go downtown to see a movie and asked me if I knew how to drive. She had a manual shift car and was nervous about driving in the city at night. I said "Yes," although I had never driven a car. I knew I could figure it out. On the way downtown, I must have stalled her car a thousand times. By the time we were driving back home, I had figured out how to work the clutch, and that is how I learned to drive. I decided I should get my driver's licence.

Back in those days, you didn't have to pass a test to get your licence. All you had to do was go to the licence bureau and swear that you had driven 400 miles without having an accident. My first thought was, "How could I have driven 400 miles if I don't have a licence?" But I was told to put my hand on the Bible and just swear I'd driven those 400 miles. That's how I got my licence. (This system remained until, one day, to prove a point, a man obtained a driver's licence for his dog. From that moment on, the government required a driver's test before awarding a licence.) Soon after, I got the use of a company car. A customer had declared bankruptcy and Peerless had a lien on his business. One of the assets was a six-month-old Ford station wagon, and I was given it to drive.

I loved the factory and couldn't wait to go to work every day, but it took me a while to figure out what "having a job" meant – I was that naive. All I had known was school and camp, and it took me some time to adjust. The first year, I actually told Moe I wanted to go back to summer camp and be a counsellor. He said, "This is a job, Alvin; not school! You don't get two months off; you get two *weeks* off."

Socially, I had a new life too. I was eighteen years old, I had a new name and a job that I loved, and a whole new world was opening up to me. However, I was a little envious of my high school friends who went on to university. I never had that experience and felt I was missing something. My friends and I were the same age but at very different stages in our lives, and I didn't fit in with them anymore. My circle of friends slowly evolved and began to include working people, who understood my new life and who I had something in common with.

When I started at Peerless, Moe told me to join the Elm Ridge Golf and Country Club and the Shaar Hashomayim Synagogue as his son. Elm Ridge was, and still is, the premier golf club of Montreal's Jewish community, and many nights after work, I would head out to Dorval to play golf. Membership was costly: I was required to make a down payment of one hundred dollars and remit an additional one hundred dollars per year for ten consecutive years. But it was worth it. I made new friends and connections at Elm Ridge that I maintain to this day. The Bronfmans, Steinbergs, Pascals, Reitmans, and other pillars of the Montreal business establishment were members, and there was a great sense of community. Joining Elm Ridge was the beginning of my networking in the Montreal Jewish community, which guided me to become involved in philanthropy many years later. Moe showed me that life isn't only about work. Today, more than sixty-five years later (and counting), I am still a member of Elm Ridge Golf and Country Club.

The first week after I started at Peerless, when I'd just received my first paycheck, two of Ralph's good friends showed up at the office. They said it was customary to donate one week's pay a year – or two per cent of your annual salary – to Federation Combined Jewish Appeal (CJA), the main Jewish charity in Montreal. I was happy to do it because I knew it was a good cause and I endorsed my first cheque to the federation. When I was still in high school I only gave fifty cents a year to the federation, but now that I was working, I knew that the following week I'd get another paycheque.

Out of the thirty-five dollars a week the company paid me, Moe Segal suggested I give ten dollars a week to my mother for running the household. The first thought that came to my mind was, "He is a very wealthy man; why does he need my ten dollars a week?" When I asked Moe about it, he said, "I want you to learn how to be responsible for yourself." When I started working at Peerless, I felt that Moe stopped treating me like a member of his immediate family and more like I was a completely independent person. Once, at the end of a family Passover holiday at a resort in the Catskill Mountains, I was packing the luggage into the car while I saw Moe checking out at the front desk. He then came up to me and asked, "Alvin, did you check out yet?" I said,

"No, I saw you checking out." He then told me, "I paid for the family, but not for you," so I had to check myself out at the front desk and pay for my stay. He never gave up showing me how to be independent and responsible for myself.

I was getting more and more comfortable in the factory, making friends with the foremen, and learning as much as I could. After my first few months, Moe must have realized from my conversations with him that the factory needed help because on 1 January 1952, he hired an engineer by the name of Sam Closner. Sam was Moe's brother-in-law's brother-in-law, and had been a wartime munitions engineer. I was told that Sam would be my new boss but almost immediately it was the other way around: I became his boss. I was never told anything; that's just how the relationship developed. Sam asked me where the problems were and what had to be done to fix them, because it was clear that I already knew what improvements were needed.

Our job was to make sure the factory ran efficiently. Peerless sold inexpensive suits, so every penny we saved on production went to the bottom line, and Sam and I worked on every detail we could think of. I loved working with the head quality foreman, Sam Kirsch, as well. He always came up with new ideas on pressing, pocket sewing, and suggestions for making other operations as quick and easy as possible.

Each operator was paid by the hour and had to produce a quota. Our challenge was to make the work easier and raise the quota. How could we save on material handling? Would a higher stool make someone's job easier and faster? When an operator sews a pocket and makes a tack at the end, a thread is left dangling. How can he cut that thread shorter so it doesn't have to be trimmed afterward? Little details like that added up. We were always looking for a faster machine, a better machine, a more streamlined system, so that we could produce more garments for less money.

I realized early on that Peerless was part of a very competitive industry controlled by the Joint Committee of the Men's and Boys' Clothing Industry in Quebec (JC). The JC was a province-wide body that regulated working conditions in the men's clothing industry. In Quebec, there were different J C s for every industry (women's dresses, women's cloaks and suits, men's and boys' suits, tourism, hotel workers, construction, etc.) and the committees were made up of representatives from both management and labour in each sector. A list of all the J C rules and regulations was printed so that every manufacturer knew what they had to follow. These decrees described types and styles of garments and their methods of production, covering every part of the manufacturing process. There were precise descriptions of each operation and their classifications, as well as rates of pay, overtime, vacation, holidays to be paid, layoffs, and all the exceptions.

J C inspectors came into each factory every three months to ensure that every individual operator's job matched its pay schedule and that the operators' salaries met the minimum rules and regulations according to the decree. The Joint Committee printed and circulated a report after every inspection of all the factories in the province. Those reports went to all the manufacturers in the industry. It was a great way to learn what your competitors were doing as the reports showed, among other things, a summary of hours worked, wages paid, and the number of employees in each factory. As a result, there were no secrets, and you had a sense of where you stood in the industry.

Meanwhile, mechanization had started transforming the industry. I kept up to date about new technologies by attending machinery shows in New York, Boston, Charlotte, North Carolina, and Atlanta. Our competitors attended these shows as well, so that helped me become familiar with the industry and the people in it: the manufacturers, innovators, consultants, and competitors. As long as there was a return on investment, I had a free hand to hire consultants I met at the shows to help us improve our systems, operations, and products. They taught me a lot about how to keep the factory efficient and up-to-date.

The factory on Pine Avenue was very crowded, so one day in 1952 I was told that Moe and Phil were moving the cutting room to a new location at 9500 St Laurent Boulevard. The new location took more than an hour to get to by car because the road north of Cremazie Boulevard was unpaved. Unfortunately, I made

2.3 The steel cutting tables in our factory today. They still haven't warped.

a big mistake when I bought cutting tables for the new location. I purchased beautiful hardwood cutting tables made of tongue-and-groove hardwood strips like a floor. The wood must not have been dry because within six months of use, they started to warp and the edges curled up. Cutting machines have to roll on a flat surface, so if the tables warp they're no good and have to be replaced. I learned from my mistake and when Peerless moved into its current location thirty-six years later, I had steel cutting tables built like ones I'd seen on a trip to Germany. I designed them and we built them in-house. They're gorgeous – the best cutting tables in the world – and steel doesn't warp.

At one point, we introduced a new system for moving bundles of work in the pants factory from station to station. Instead of having a "floor boy" pick up the bundles and move them to the next station, we brought in the Singer Truck System – a square cart on wheels. It made moving the work from one operator to the other much easier and eliminated the need for the floor boy. However, getting the new system running efficiently meant rearranging some of the sewing-machine stations, which I did.

Around the same time, I heard about a retired designer who had formerly worked for Rubin Brothers in Victoriaville, a manufacturer of high-priced fine clothing. Since we were still having problems with the collars, I decided to bring him in as a consultant to try and fix the collar issue. The first sample that he made, the collar fit perfectly.

One weekend soon after both these changes were made, I got called off the golf course at Elm Ridge. It was a Saturday and, in those days, when they sent a cart out to get you off the course, it was usually because someone had passed away. I was told to get home because Moe wanted to see me. When I walked into the den, Moe and Harry Diamond were there. I had always tried to keep Harry informed of the changes I was making, but he'd never seemed interested. Now Harry said, "Alvin just put in a handling system to move around the work and it's no good."

Moe asked, "Alvin, is that true?"

I said I did put it in and added, "Harry, if there's an improvement we can make, believe me, come in Monday morning and we'll fix it together."

That Monday, Harry came in, sat on a stool, and got the mechanic and me to move the sewing machines around to where he said they should be to make best use of the new truck system. Finally, we finished, and Harry and I both realized his new layout was exactly as I had had it before. I didn't say a word.

The next day, Harry came into the front office and told Moe, "I cannot work with Alvin. Either he goes or I go."

Moe didn't hesitate for a second. "Take your hat and coat. Goodbye, Harry."

So after twenty-eight years, Harry Diamond left Peerless. Moe, Phil, and I were left standing there, and I didn't know what to say. Moe told me, "Alvin, you're now in charge of the factory."

I'd been at Peerless for less than three years, and since the first day having a great time learning, solving problems, and helping people. Now, suddenly, having just turned twenty-one, I was put in charge officially. Moe and Phil wanted to tell all the foremen that I was in charge. I wasn't ready to hear that; I panicked and started

Tel. PLateau 9166

ALVIN SEGAL
ASSISTANT DIRECTOR
IN CHARGE OF
METHODS · TIME STUDY · PRODUCTION
COST CONTROL

Manufacturing Division of
PEERLESS CLOTHING MFG. CO.
Canada's Best Value in Clothing

55 PINE AVENUE E.   MONTREAL

2.4 My first business card. I hadn't been given a title at Peerless so I made one up for myself, along with a list of my responsibilities.

to cry. "No! Please don't call them in," I pleaded. I looked at Moe and Phil. "They already know I'm in charge of the factory."

There's a Yiddish word: *bashert*. It means "fate and destiny." I've always thought the events that took me from failing in high school to running a men's suit factory contained a heavy dose of *bashert*.

3

Taking Ownership of the Factory

When Moe and Phil put me in charge of the factory, I started working at a new level even though my job hadn't really changed. This had nothing to do with a title because I didn't have one, and only I knew I was officially in charge. It wasn't about money – I don't think I even got a raise. Still, I felt I had to take myself to a new level of responsibility. I felt more accountable and, maybe because Harry had left, I also felt unleashed and able to run things with no interference. I was an employee "taking ownership" of the factory. I finally knew what my job was.

I realize now that the events that took place at Peerless during the years that followed were necessary for the company to survive. When I started at Peerless, the company had no direction; no one was really in charge. Moe was semiretired, Phil was trying to recover from his heart attack and still wasn't working full time, and Hershey was trying to keep it together but had one foot out the door. His dream had always been to go into retail, to get out of the family business and do his own thing. Eventually, when his father returned to work, Hershey went back to school, graduated, and ended up founding the clothing retailer Le Château.

One day I would be told by the office to raise production and the next day I was asked to lower it. I was called into the office, and they would ask me to find ways to make a cheaper garment and then would turn around a few days later and ask for higher quality garments. It seemed like every time a customer made a complaint, the policy of the company changed. I became involved very quickly with everything that had to do with manufacturing, from the boiler room to the shipping room. Slowly but surely, everybody started calling me for every little problem that came up. When something broke in the building, whether it was electrical or mechanical, I would be called to get it fixed. I became involved not only in the factory but with everything else in the company except the office.

One day I was called to the reception and was introduced to a salesman, David Abony, who had just moved to Canada with his family. David had been an architect in his country, but while waiting for his licence in Canada was working as a salesman for an equipment company. He came to Peerless to introduce a new kind of racking system for our shipping room. When he showed it to me I saw that he didn't really understand his product, but I did right away, and we bought it. I installed it myself with David's help. I remember climbing like a monkey to the top of the new rack to make sure it was installed properly. It came out so beautifully that we changed all the racking in our shipping room. It streamlined the look of our shipping room and made it more efficient. That racking system is still used to this day everywhere in the industry.

I became very friendly with David and at that point often thought about leaving Peerless and going into the real estate business with him as a partner. I saw no real future for myself at Peerless – even though I was in charge of the factory I was still only an employee, and real estate was in the back of my mind as a long-term plan.

Through my work in the factory, I learned a lot. I don't think there was ever a dull moment at Peerless; every day in a factory is different from the one before. You never knew what was going to happen: what operator wasn't going to show up to work and what machine was going to break down. One interesting learning experience came about when I wanted to hire a new foreman. The man I selected had a contract with his employer and he was afraid to break it. He wanted to accept my offer to work at Peerless, so he hired a lawyer to help extricate him from his contract. His lawyer advised him, "Start showing up late for work and start making

3.1 The racking system, which is still used in the industry today.

mistakes. If you're lucky, you might get fired." That was exactly what happened, and not long afterward I was able to hire him. I learned that contracts are only good for the employee and not for the employer. So much for employment contracts.

I was developing a good relationship with the head foreman of the pants shop, Thomas Konningstal, and his assistant, Mendel Unikowsky. Mendel had one operation that required five employees to complete. I once asked him, "Mendel, why do you put five employees of different nationalities to work on this one operation?" His answer taught me a lesson that I've never forgotten: "If they are all from different nationalities and speak different languages, they won't talk and will concentrate on their work." I always followed that lesson and it is actually one of the reasons why the sectoral union was never able to organize us. The union could never sell their so-called advantages and benefits in any consistent manner to our culturally diverse employees. Today, we have almost sixty different cultural communities and numerous languages spoken in our factory. Thomas was a very smart man, for whom I had a lot of respect, and we became very close friends. He stayed with me until he retired, many years later.

Before the Second World War, the sectoral unions had taken over most of the men's fine-tailored clothing industry in Montreal, and in the 1950s, when I arrived at Peerless, the Amalgamated Clothing Workers of America (ACWA) exercised great influence in the industry. One of the things I learned from going to trade shows and interacting with other people in the industry was that there were innovations our competitors couldn't adopt because of their membership in the ACWA. "Sectoral" means there is one master contract applied to all companies under that union, and no single company can change the contract. Peerless's competitors who were members of the sectoral union couldn't take advantage of technological change without renegotiating the sectoral contract, and the union rarely let that happen. Peerless's main advantage has always been staying out of the sectoral union.

Moe Segal understood that the unions were crippling the operations of his competitors, so he made sure his workers were satisfied and wouldn't feel tempted to unionize. He always said this was one of the reasons for his success and that made sense to me, not just from a bottom-line point of view but because the workers at Peerless were happy with the deal they had. Not only did all Peerless factory employees have Jewish holidays off (with pay after five years seniority) but also an annual Christmas bonus, free life insurance, and a major medical plan.

Not being part of the sectoral union gave us the advantage of being able to adopt new technology, making production more efficient and saving money, and was the foundation of why we were so successful then and why we still are today. Nowadays, since we have only a few Jewish people left working in the factory, we work on Jewish holidays. However, we pay our factory employees double time for those days. Today the non-Jewish employees look forward to Jewish holidays and often know when those dates are coming before I do.

I realized right away that the benefits given by Peerless were very important to the factory employees. In the spring of 1952 I experienced my first "cabane à sucre" party, organized by the employees and paid for by Peerless. (A cabane à sucre is a traditional Québécois celebration where sap collected from maple trees is boiled down to syrup.) The same spring, I participated in the Peerless annual softball game. Peerless had its own hockey team as well, and every 1 July on Canada Day we had a company picnic at a beach called Plage Laval. Those experiences never left me, and paved the way to my connection with my workers. Keeping these feelings alive became an obsession of mine, and well over sixty-five years later, even with our changed workforce, I not only try to maintain that same atmosphere but over the years have added some new traditions.

At the end of 1952, I started hearing about employees who had been working at Peerless for more than twenty years. I took it upon myself to find a way to recognize them and thought an engraved watch would be a great idea. I found a jewelry store on St Laurent Boulevard, near the factory, and met the owner, Charles Bedzow, who sold me solid gold watches for one hundred dollars each. I had "Twenty Years Loyal Service" engraved on the back of the watches and gave them out as presents to employees at our annual Christmas party. That event still goes on today and is extremely meaningful to everyone at Peerless. Although the watches are no longer solid gold, it's the thought that counts. Over the years, I've handed out more than a thousand watches – a staggering number of sixty in 2014 alone. At the annual Christmas party in 1971, the employees gave me a Mickey Mouse watch to mark my twenty years at Peerless. They decorated the hall with banners thanking me for the way the company was progressing. I must admit that every year, it's an emotional experience for me to share the excitement and pride with our employees. Through the years, we've added bonuses for ten, twenty, thirty, and forty years of service. When I finally retire, it will be difficult for anyone to replace the friendships I've nurtured with my employees. I hope the example I have set continues for years to come.

When I joined the company in 1951 our annual sales were about two million dollars, all from low-end synthetic suits. There were two basic styles of suits, single-breasted and double-breasted, made mostly of rayon fabric, and they came in four different colours – navy, black, grey, and taupe. The fabrics were purchased from several Canadian textile mills. At that time, Peerless used no

3.2 Here I am handing out watches at a Peerless factory
Christmas party in the early 1960s.

imported fabrics. If a suit with two pairs of pants retailed for
$19.95, we sold it for $10. (Usually, the retailer doubles the price
they paid at wholesale; it's called "keystoning.")

For two million in sales, we never made more than five-per-cent
profit or $100,000. A good, efficient operation was happy to
make that kind of margin. Peerless never manufactured according to the orders that came in; we just manufactured suits for
stock, kept the factory running, and kept inventory in the shipping room ready for sale. In those days, at the end of March, we
stopped making suits and started making overcoats and station-
wagon coats (a trench coat with an imitation fur collar) for the

fall and winter season. We made overcoats from April to August, and that's all we had in the shipping room. When September came, we switched back to suits.

Back in those days, all that was needed to start a men's clothing business was to buy and install a cutting table – in other words, do your own cutting – send the sewing and pressing work out to a contractor, and do your own shipping. In 1957, according to the Joint Committee's report on the men's clothing industry, there were seventy-five cutting rooms in Quebec, eighty-four manufacturers of men's suits and 108 manufacturers of odd pants. The apparel industry in Montreal was booming. It was like the Detroit automobile business in the 1950s. There was no shortage of jobs and companies were in hiring mode. If you were willing to work in a factory, you could make a wage and feed your family. It was a very competitive industry.

When I was put in charge of the factory in the fall of 1954, my job was not only to ensure things ran as smoothly and cost-effectively as possible, but also to deal with the JC, whose main task was to monitor our wages and working conditions. All companies – unionized and nonunionized – had to comply with the JC's decrees. The system of Joint Committees across the province had been adopted from France and brought to Quebec by Premier Maurice Duplessis in the 1930s. He thought it would be more difficult for unions to organize if wages and working conditions were the same in nonunionized and unionized factories. Nonetheless, most of the companies in the men's apparel sector in Montreal (except for Peerless and a few others) were taken over by the big international sectoral unions. They supported the JC system because they didn't want nonunionized shops to have an unfair advantage.

The Joint Committee representatives were divided equally into two groups – labour and management – representing various subsectors of the men's and boys' apparel industry, from non-union men's pants, to cotton jeans, to fine tailored suits, to men's outerwear, etc. The unions had no choice but to sit on the JC as members, which was ironic because the JC never helped the union movement; it was invented to neutralize them. The Joint Committee was funded through a payroll levy on all employees and employers. Every year the JC published a list of all companies that included a summary of employee hours worked, total salaries, average wages, and wage breakdowns. That was useful information for everybody, including the unions, because everyone could use it to see what their competitors were doing. The committee met twice a month, and there was typically a lot of discussion about who was trying to bend the rules and get away with something. It was embarrassing for the offenders, but useful information for everybody else at the table.

There was a period during the fifties and sixties when it was almost a science to keep labour costs as low as possible within the JC's regulations. Employers would try anything to reduce labour costs. Every operation in the factory had a different classification schedule: cutting, pressing, sleeve setting, pocket making, lining making, and so on, and each classification had a minimum hourly wage. The JC minimum wage was ten to twenty cents more than Quebec's minimum wage, but you could always start a new operator as an apprentice working at the provincial minimum. New employees would have to be "gradually promoted" (every three months) to the Joint Committee's minimum pay for that operation, but the money saved was sufficient that some companies hired nothing but apprentices.

Every company was allowed a certain number of apprentices, but they could never make up more than twenty per cent of the total number of factory employees. If the percentage of apprentices rose above the twenty percent allowed, the Joint Committee made us gradually promote them to match the JC minimum wage for the job they were doing. Every three months we were required to make retroactive pay adjustments if we had too many apprentices. The Joint Committee was responsible to the Quebec Department of Labour, and its mandate was to enforce the JC decree. Every three months, the JC inspectors would come into the factory, go to each and every operator, and ask, "What operation are you doing?" "How much are you paid?" "How many hours do you work?" The inspectors would monitor everything; they had a lot of authority. Companies spent a lot of time and energy trying to figure out how to get around the rules of the JC, but it was impossible in the men's clothing sector.

I wanted to put in a piecework incentive system in order to give the operators the chance to earn more money based on their individual productivity. This system would have allowed Peerless to raise its production and lower its costs, but Moe Segal told me, "No, not as long as I own the company. It's too difficult to monitor and control."

My dream was to get a position on the JC board because the JC schedule of minimum rates was the same whether you made low-priced or high-priced suits, which didn't seem fair. It didn't make sense to me that high quality worsted-wool suits and our synthetic fabric machine-made garments were subject to the same rules and regulations with the same minimum rates. On the JC board, Peerless and all other nonunionized shops were represented by a fellow named Jack Rabinovitch, who was the son-in-law of the owner of Society Brand Clothing, a manufacturer of high priced worsted-wool suits. I became friendly with Jack and when Society Brand was taken over by the Amalgamated union, his seat on the committee became available. There was nobody on the Joint Committee representing the lower-priced machine-made product. If I could get a seat on the board, maybe I could change things.

I approached the Quebec Government and advised them of my interest in representing the nonunionized shops on the JC board, and in 1964, I was finally invited by the government to sit on the committee as a member. I became the representative of the independent nonaffiliated (nonunion) manufacturers, which at that time included Peerless and a few small manufacturers. All the other manufacturers at the table were under the sectoral Amalgamated union. That seat on the JC would eventually be pivotal to my future in the men's fine clothing industry and would lead me to a very influential position affecting the entire Canadian apparel industry.

During those years, mechanization was slowly taking over the industry and a company called Reece Buttonhole introduced an automatic pocket-making machine. All that an operator had to do was load the parts of the pocket into the machine; they didn't even have to know how to sew and the machine would produce a pocket. Under the JC, pocket-making was a Class A job, with

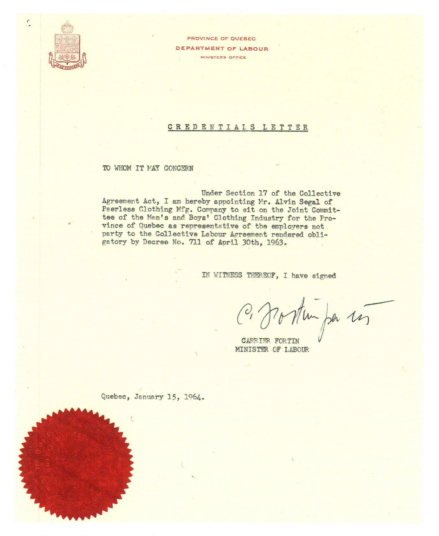

PROVINCE OF QUEBEC
DEPARTMENT OF LABOUR
MINISTER'S OFFICE

C R E D E N T I A L S   L E T T E R

TO WHOM IT MAY CONCERN

                Under Section 17 of the Collective
Agreement Act, I am hereby appointing Mr. Alvin Segal of
Peerless Clothing Mfg. Company to sit on the Joint Committee of the Men's and Boys' Clothing Industry for the Province of Quebec as representative of the employers not
party to the Collective Labour Agreement rendered obli-
gatory by Decree No. 711 of April 30th, 1963.

                IN WITNESS THEREOF, I have signed

                      CARRIER FORTIN
                      MINISTER OF LABOUR

Quebec, January 15, 1964.

3.3 The Quebec Department of Labour appointed me to the JC on 15 January 1964. Back then the province still corresponded in English.

the highest minimum rate of pay. It didn't make sense to continue paying the higher rate to the same person who was now just loading a machine. As a result, I asked that the JC introduce a new classification for making pockets with an automatic machine. The new operation was classified at the lowest wage level in the JC schedule. I had the flexibility to take advantage of that machine because we didn't have to deal with the sectoral union.

Stan Kivenko and I sat on the Joint Committee together for more than thirty years, until the system was abolished. Stan, who was partners with his brother in Jack Spratt Inc., represented the men's jeans sector of the industry. Since we were both nonunionized, we looked out for each other on the committee and often rolled our eyes at the same time in meetings. At two meetings a month, one general and one executive, with the inspectors reporting back on what they found at the other shops, we learned everything that was going on in our sectors. As Stan recently recalled:

Alvin and I were the only technical people sitting on the Joint Committee who knew how to make our products down to the smallest detail. We both had the most modern, technologically advanced shops in Canada, if not North America. We both would travel to the trade shows together, and we were always updating our plants. We attempted to make sure that the Joint Committee had their decrees aligned properly with the way we made our product. Alvin naturally wanted the decree to reflect how he operated and I wanted the same for jeans. In a jean there were thirty-three operations, in pants forty-five, and in men's jackets over one hundred. They tried to define every single operation and they had umpteen different categories, even for a machine operator doing different operations on the same kind of machine. The result was that the shop was totally inflexible. Operators could always move down to a lower skill but we still had to pay them at the higher wage.

One of the seats on the committee was held by the head of the Amalgamated union, whose representative was always telling me how much he'd like to organize Peerless's employees. In response, I would tell him, "As far as I know, my employees don't want to lose the benefits they have now – paid Jewish holidays and Christmas bonuses."

During the 1940s, when Moe was fending off the unions, one of his strategies had been to pick a key operator in every section – sleeve setters, lining sewers – and make that person an executive with a guaranteed forty-hour work-week. As executives, these operators couldn't join a union. Peerless had a glut of executives, but it worked. If there was ever a strike, we could keep production going with our "executives." It was a brilliant move.

During my time as manager of the factory, I made sure that we matched whatever the unions had settled on in their sectoral contract negotiations. In the fifties, operators were paid less than a dollar an hour, and that rate increased every year. The system was that whatever the Amalgamated union won, the JC would incorporate into their decrees within a year. That was fine with us; whatever the union increase was we paid right away, so that our employees had no incentive to join the union. I always made sure I was fair with our employees and never gave them a reason to join a union. This was very important because it gave me the flexibility to make changes needed to increase our productivity. If we put in new technology, I made sure the employees shared in the benefits it produced.

The Joint Committee's agenda focused on the smallest details you could imagine. During the 1960s, there was a full-blown crisis when unisex clothing came into fashion. Was it men's wear? Was it ladies' wear? This was a crucial question, because there was a separate Joint Committee for ladies' wear with their own inspectors and rate schedules. For a very brief period, I started to manufacture ladies' skirts. In men's suits, the fabric might change or there might be a slight difference in lapel size from one season to the next, but you're basically manufacturing the same template on an assembly line year after year. Ladies' fashion changes from season to season, and that makes it almost an entirely different business. We had to maintain a separate record of how many hours the operators worked on men's clothing and how many on ladies', because each had a different hourly minimum. It became very confusing. By the mid-nineties, it eventually led to the abolishment of the Joint Committee – a change which I encouraged, as I believed it would make the apparel industry more flexible.

For all my complaints about the Joint Committee and the bureaucracy it imposed, I learned more about the business I was in than I ever would have without it. Between the inspectors' reports every three months and the annual report they issued to the industry (which nobody read but me), I always knew what problems the competition was dealing with, what inroads they were making, where and how to stay a step ahead of the game.

In those years, each garment was rated by the industry for retail purposes. Our garments were machine-made and rated accordingly. On a scale of one to six, a top-of-the-line tailored Samuelsohn suit was rated a six. Peerless was a one or even lower, an X, because our company manufactured at the lowest price possible: two sleeves, a lapel, and a collar that didn't fit. I was curious about what the competition was up to, so I'd go on reconnaissance missions to Eaton's and other stores. Peerless suits were selling in the bargain basement but I'd venture up to the second floor where the prices were higher, and I'd find what were basically the same suits, except they were more expensive. We couldn't sell upstairs because Peerless suits had no hand tailoring and we used the wrong fabrics. We just had to accept that we were stuck with that number one rating. This made me want to learn about marketing and merchandising in order to achieve a better rating and higher selling prices.

I noticed in our pants shop that the operators making the pockets couldn't pick up the pocketing fabric because it was too slippery. I told Moe, "It's slowing us down." He said, "Alvin, from now on, you buy the pocketing from whomever you want." So I bought it from a new supplier and we solved the pocketing problem and ended up saving money as well. That's when I started becoming immersed in the ins and outs of trimmings – thread, pocketing, linings, interlinings, buttons, zippers – and how we could save time and money on them. This would lead me to a whole new aspect of manufacturing men's fine clothing.

One day, one of our suppliers, Eli Yaffe, came to me and said, "The Vietnam War is coming, there's going to be a shortage of brass zippers [brass preceded the nylon zippers]. You'd better stock up, Alvin." I had seen shortages during the Second World War, so I bought two years' supply of zippers – rolls and rolls of them. When the front office saw the inventory, they asked me what on earth we were doing with so many zippers. When the war didn't cause a run on brass zippers, I learned about excess inventory from that mistake.

One day, Moe saw me in the shipping room and asked, "Alvin, what are you doing here?" I told him that everything was going well in the factory, so I was just taking a look around in shipping. He said that there was always something to do in the factory and that was where I belonged. At that moment, I realized that the factory was a mystery to the Segal family, who didn't know how to deal with it and didn't want to learn. The factory and the office were two separate entities, and since I was in charge of the factory, nobody thought I should get involved with the rest of the business. After Moe left for the day, I was back in the shipping room, looking around and asking questions, because that's where we got feedback from our customers.

Back then, my main job was to keep manufacturing costs down. The office kept track of costs; they took the total production and divided it by the total payroll to get a cost per garment. Anything I could do to lower that number went right to our bottom line. I started analyzing the trimming costs in detail. I spent three months breaking them down, item by item, to get a more precise understanding of the real costs before presenting my findings to Moe, who looked at my report for about two seconds before tearing it up into little pieces. "Never tell anyone your real true costs," he said. My detailed costing was two cents off the number he was working from. According to Moe, you should keep your true costs secret (particularly from your salesmen) and always pad the number a little bit to leave room for the unforeseen. It was an invaluable lesson, and I still follow it to this day.

One of the ways I managed to cut costs was to bring the manufacture of canvas fronts in-house. Every men's suit jacket has a canvas front between the lining and the shell fabric, as an inner support fabric to help it keep its shape and hang properly. When I started in the business, we ordered from a canvas front maker. We were paying a dollar for each canvas front, which was expensive. I did some research and told Moe that Peerless could save money if we made the fronts ourselves. Moe said, "Try it." In order to do that, I'd have to buy both the fabric and the machines.

The canvas front makers and suit manufacturers belonged to the same Amalgamated union and had a cozy arrangement with

Canada Hair Cloth, the only supplier of material for canvas fronts in Canada. When I contacted them to buy the fabric, they refused to sell the fabric to me. At that time, Singer was the only supplier of the zigzag sewing machine – the needle jumped from side to side – and you needed a zigzag machine to make canvas fronts. When I tried to order the sewing machines from Singer they wouldn't sell them to me either, because I wasn't a canvas front maker. Canada Hair Cloth seemed to control everything.

I found a way to make the canvas fronts on my own. I bought used zigzag machines from a second-hand dealer and I imported jute and canvas fabrics. When I tried to bring the shipment into the country, however, it was stopped at customs, and I was asked to pay a high import tariff on both fabrics. Who was the government protecting with the tariff on jute? There was no jute fabric being made in Canada. Canada Hair Cloth was one of the players in Canada's textile monopoly that I was just starting to get acquainted with. After a lot of negotiating, we ended up paying the tariffs, the shipment was cleared, and we started making canvas fronts in our factory.

That incident gave me the drive to one day challenge the monopoly of the Canadian Textile Institute (CTI). Moe told me that Peerless's profit on the whole year was equal to the fifty cents a suit I'd saved with those canvas fronts. The company that had been making our canvas fronts went out of business soon after.

I was always curious about how to improve our operation, and sometimes called consultants in to help us because there was nobody on the management side at Peerless with any manufacturing knowledge. There was one consulting firm called Kurt Salmon Associates (KSA) that I kept hiring to advise me on what I needed to know about new machines and how they could improve our factory and the quality of our products. By this time, I was involved with all major decisions. If the office wanted to raise production because sales got a few extra orders, or lower production because they'd lost an order, it had to go through me. I gained invaluable experience and responsibility at an early age.

In those first five years, I attended night classes in the commerce program at what was then Sir George Williams College – now

Concordia University. I took classes on labour relations, industrial relations, and quality control. While my classmates took
notes and memorized facts they had no way of applying in the
real world, I audited the courses and tried to use everything I was
learning on the factory floor and in our dealings with the Joint
Committee. I was often exhausted, but it was well worth it.
Between my work on the JC and what I was learning at night,
I was expanding my knowledge of the men's apparel industry,
where our company was positioned, and what my role was, all of
which would serve me well in the upheaval to come.

4

Change Is in the Air

In the spring of 1956, almost four and a half years after I started working at Peerless, my mother, Betty, passed away. We had been told two years earlier by Dr Martin Hoffman at the Jewish General Hospital that she had breast cancer and probably had two years to live, and that was precisely what happened. During the last two years of her life she had several operations, but the end was inevitable and very sad. I was at the hospital, by her side, when she took her last breath. My mother was fifty-two years old when she died; I was twenty-two years old and had just lost my best friend.

Two weeks after my mother's death, Phil Segal, Moe's brother and business partner, also passed away. Phil had been ill for almost five years with a heart condition and diabetes. He was fifty-five when he passed. Moe, who had probably been miserable for the two years that my mother had been ill, was a widower once again and at the same time lost his brother and business partner. I can only assume that he was in a state of shock.

Phil had left his fifty per cent of the business equally to his three sons, Ralph, Hershey, and Moey, giving each a little over sixteen per cent of the company. Moe, however, was the sole executor of his brother Phil's estate and now had total control of Peerless. Almost immediately he said he wanted to sell the company. I asked him why, and told him that I could keep running the factory and that he could stay semiretired. In those days, the strength of the company was basically the factory. Looking back, Moe must have realized that the company needed to be more than just the factory and that a major change in management was required for it to flourish and succeed, but he didn't want to do it himself. He wanted to sell Peerless to his younger brother, Hy, and keep the company in his family. For years, Moe had been the patriarch of the family, with everyone coming to him with their problems. He would always help anyone who asked. Now he couldn't wait to get out.

Moe brought Hy into the company from P. Segal Co. (the Peerless boys' wear division). He decided to pay Hy a salary of $125,000 a year to manage the company, learn what was going on, and to support the purchase of Peerless. In 1956, a salary of that size was more than enough. For three or four years Hy tried to create a management team consisting of employees already working in the company. He would call meetings with our head shipper, our Toronto salesman, and our head merchandiser – everyone with a title, including me. Hy would go around the table and ask, "How many shares do you want?" One guy would say, "I'll take five per cent." Another would say, "I'd like ten per cent." It was ridiculous. Then, Hy would turn to me and ask, "Alvin, what do you want?" and I'd say I didn't want anything to do with it. I knew they didn't know how to run the company. In fact, none of them knew anything about running the business or the factory. Even at twenty-three years old, I felt that being in business with them would never work out.

Although Moe had promised to sell the company to Hy, he realized that Hy couldn't take ownership of Peerless alone but thought Hy would be able to assemble the people needed. Hy was missing a factory partner in order to complete his team, but I wouldn't change my mind. Without proper management and partners who already knew the factory, it would be very hard for Hy to keep the business going forward. When Moe realized Hy wasn't coming to him with a plan to buy Peerless, he started travelling all over North America trying to sell the company, but he never found a buyer. In the meantime, Hershey was still trying to run the company part-time with Hy, while Ralph was becoming more involved. I was still running the factory. No one really knew what was going on, but the company kept going, only downhill. I was always thinking of my future and considered leaving. Peerless couldn't survive the way it was being run. Something had to happen.

Within a year of my mother's death, Moe married his third wife, Adah Ballon, a family acquaintance. Adah had no children, and my sisters and I were very happy when she came into our lives. Adah became very close to all three of us. Moe and Adah continued travelling and spending their winters in Florida while the company went from bad to worse without any real management.

After lunch one Friday, Hershey came to me and said, "Alvin, I need a favour. I promised a young lady I would drive her up north for a ski weekend, but I'm so tired I would like to leave now and just go home. Could you please pick her up, and drive her to my place in St Sauveur?" I agreed, and after dinner I picked up Hershey's young lady friend, Sandra Herman, and drove her up north. Sandra and I hit it off immediately; we laughed and joked all the way to Hershey's house. We had a great time together and planned to go skiing the next day at Mont Tremblant. The next day, I met Hershey and his two friends, Otto Sand and Oscar Rajsky, who had had arrived from Montreal early that morning. Little did I know that I'd meet Otto and Oscar again later in life, and they would each play an important part in my future.

Otto, Oscar, and Hershey were great skiers, so they went to the expert hills and left Sandra and me alone. We spent the entire day skiing, talking, and joking, getting to know each other. Saturday night, Sandra and I spent more time together; we ate, drank, and just had a good time. On Sunday morning, I drove Sandra back home to Montreal. We got along so well that weekend that I decided she was the girl I wanted to marry. Even then, when I knew what I wanted, I had a tendency to act quickly. She was the nicest Jewish girl I had ever met.

I wanted to meet her parents right away. Since they would be leaving the following week on a three-month business trip to Europe, I was invited to their home for dinner the next Friday night. I really liked her family, and soon afterwards Sandra and I decided to get engaged, planning to marry within six months. Her father gave me two choices; he told me he'd either pay for a

MR. AND MRS. ALVIN SEGAL, whose marriage took place recently at the Shaare Zion Synagogue. The bride is the former Miss Sandra Herman, daughter of Mr. and Mrs. Moses Herman of Hampstead. Mr. Segal is the son of Mr. Moe Segal and the late Mrs. Segal of Montreal.

4.1 The wedding announcement for Sandra and me, 1957.

big wedding or give us a small ceremony and $10,000. We chose to have a big wedding and were married by Rabbi Maurice Cohen on 5 September 1957 at Shaare Zion Congregation on Côte St Luc Road. The wedding was beautiful, but when the evening was over I realized I should probably have taken the $10,000, since I had nothing in the bank and now had to support a wife. That's what happens when you get married at twenty-three years old; you would rather have a big party than think about the future.

A little over a year later we had our first daughter, Barbara, born on 28 September 1958. Seventeen months after that, our second daughter, Renee, was born on 17 February 1960, and our son, Joel, arrived on 28 December 1962. Sandra was not only the mother of my children but my best friend and confidante, and a great sounding board for all my trials and tribulations. She kept up her education, eventually getting a master's degree at McGill University, and went on to become a lawyer with both civil and common law degrees. She certainly helped me in the twenty-five years we were together.

The year after we were married, Sandra and I bought a triplex on Isabella Avenue near St Mary's hospital. I had $2,000 available for a down payment, and I took out first and second mortgages. I had no money in the bank at the time and asked Moe if he thought I was making the right decision. He said, "If you put pressure on yourself, it will make you work harder. You have a good job. I'm sure you'll find a way to make it work."

Although things were tumultuous at work, the sixties were happy years in my personal life. I had a good marriage, three beautiful children, and was developing a great circle of friends. My relationship with my Jewish faith was getting richer and included our decision to send our children to the Jewish day school. My environment – being a member of Elm Ridge Golf and Country Club, of Shaar Hashomayim synagogue, and an active member of the Jewish community – developed very positively in the 1960s.

Nine years after I joined the club, Elm Ridge moved from Dorval to Île Bizard, a small island off the western tip of Montreal on Lake of Two Mountains. Back then Île Bizard was considered the countryside, since it wasn't very developed and there weren't any highways to get there. Because the new location was an hour away from Montreal, a small group of Elm Ridge members, Ralph and I included, decided to build country homes on the island. Ralph built a real house, and I bought a prefab house (and sixteen hammers). After work, with the help of some of the pressers from the factory, I would go to Île Bizard and we'd work on putting it together; they did the hammering and I made the hamburgers for dinner. My house was finished in two weeks. My children have great memories of spending their summers at that house – which is still there today.

After the school year, both Ralph's family and mine would move out to Île Bizard for the summer, our homes next to each another. Ralph was the closest Segal to me, and our wives and children got to know each other better. Our children spent a lot of time together. On the weekends and on warm summer evenings, I would often take all the children out on my speedboat or canoe, and we would spend hours enjoying Lake of Two Mountains together.

Meanwhile, Hershey had left Peerless, and his brother Ralph became more involved with Hy in the financial side of the business. A good friend of Hy's, Larry Lovell, a commissioned salesman for Quebec City and the Ottawa Valley, was promoted to sales manager. Ralph, Larry, and I really handled the day-to-day operations of the company.

At one point, I overheard that the insurance company had decided to cancel our business-interruption policy and that we couldn't find a new underwriter. Peerless was in bad shape. Hy kept trying to put together a management group that made sense. The problem was that they needed a factory partner, someone on the inside of the operation, and that was me, but I kept saying no. I had learned enough by that time to know how to run things, and I knew that Hy was not getting anywhere. My stand on Hy's offer caused problems with the Segal family, who asked why I kept refusing to be part of Hy's group, saying that I wasn't even a "real" Segal. "Because I know it will never work," I said. "If you don't like it, fire me. After all, I'm only an employee here!" I think they never fired me because they knew I was the only one who really understood the factory and, at that time, there was no one on the management team with the expertise to hire a suitable replacement for me. In effect, the factory was the only department that was properly managed.

Down the hall from our cutting room at 9500 St Laurent Boulevard was another men's suit company called Towne Hall Clothes. They had a little lunch counter, Bunny's, where I would often have lunch with my friend Arthur Levitt. The Levitts were Segal family cousins. Arthur and his father owned Towne Hall

Clothes and ran the company together, but Arthur's father had just passed away. Over our lunches I would tell Arthur how bad things were at Peerless, and one day he made me an offer. He needed a partner and thought I'd be a great asset. He said, "Alvin, I'll give you half the company, and you can run the factory." I didn't know if he was serious, but it triggered my imagination.

I didn't see any future with Peerless. The company had no leader and Hy hadn't been able to put a group together to manage it. To me, the company was in shambles, so I told Moe Segal, "I'm leaving. I have another opportunity." Moe understood why I wanted to leave but said, "You're the only one who knows the factory. Why don't you wait until the company is sold and see what happens?" It finally dawned on me that I was an essential part of the business.

After three years Hy still hadn't come up with a group that could run the company without me. His anger at me for not joining him kept building and there was tension every day. In order for the company to survive, I knew something had to happen and the impasse finally gave me the idea to form my own group to buy Peerless. I knew Moe was willing to guarantee the company line of credit for two years, and that gave me added confidence to come up with my own plan; I felt like I could save the company since I was running the factory on my own with no help from anyone. It struck me that the two people best suited to take over Peerless with me were Ralph and Larry, since they were already running the outside of the business. I spoke to our auditor, Norman Cohen from Richter, who introduced me to a lawyer named Jack Shayne to see if we could work out a deal. I knew absolutely nothing about the legalities or the financing, but I knew that if I could put together a group to buy Moe out it would work, because I ran the factory and, at that point, the factory was the company. All I wanted was what I had wanted from the first day I walked into Peerless: to keep doing my job.

One stormy day, Ralph, Larry Lovell, and I flew to New York for a fashion show. It was a scary flight and was delayed due to a plane crash at LaGuardia but, after three attempts, we finally landed. The airport terminal was closed because of the plane crash, and we had to walk about a mile in the snow to find a taxi. The next day, Ralph stayed behind while Larry and I went to the airport to return home, but all the flights were cancelled due to the big snowstorm. The clerk told us we'd have to stay overnight and could leave on the first flight the next morning. A fellow standing in line behind us, George Wall, offered his hospitality for the night since he lived close by. Larry and I took George's offer. We started talking and got along very well. I quickly found out George was an insurance consultant and had been on his way to Montreal to visit clients. I saw this as a good omen and asked George to help us out with the insurance issues we had at Peerless. He did us a favour (George dealt with larger companies than Peerless) and helped us find an underwriter who solved our insurance problems. Little did I know that the changes he made in our company's coverage would be of tremendous benefit years later. George became another good friend and one of my advisors.

With advice from my new friend, George Wall, my auditor, Norman Cohen, and my lawyer, Jack Shayne, I was able to come up with a plan to buy Peerless Clothing from Moe. The hitch was that I didn't have total confidence in either Larry or Ralph, and I couldn't run Peerless all by myself. Although I was close to Ralph and his family, he and Larry were even closer. Larry could convince Ralph of anything, and that worried me. I knew that Larry didn't understand the product like I did, and that he wasn't a businessman. I knew neither of them were doing their jobs properly but I thought I would be able to influence them to make the modifications Peerless needed if it were to survive, because we would be working as a team. Since I was putting the group together and knew the factory so well, I had my own ideas about what product we should make and how we should sell it. I believed that if we bought the proper fabric and made the right styles, we could sell our suits because I knew where our product was positioned in the market. I also thought that we should start making wool suits at the retailer's opening price point. I had ideas not just about how to keep Peerless going but about how to change and improve things as well. There was no shortage of new fabrics and I wanted to take advantage of the ideas the textile mills were showing us. I knew we had room to move up a notch in wool blends.

The only way I could get my foot in the door was to become a minority partner. The plan was that Larry and I would form a partnership agreement and together would buy Moe's half of the company. Ralph, who already owned a small part, would buy the remaining shares from his two brothers: Hershey, who had already moved on to his own company, and Moey, who was sixteen years old and not really interested in the business anyway. Ralph would own fifty per cent of the company, would run the administration, and be the president. Larry and I would run sales and the factory and would own the other half of the company together.

My biggest concern was that Larry and Ralph would join forces against me because that's how things worked in the day-to-day running of the company. To solve that problem, Jack Shayne introduced me to what was called a "shotgun clause" as part of my partnership agreement with Larry. With that clause in our contract we could sell only to each other. I had the right to refuse any offer Larry made and then the right to buy him out at the same price he'd offered, plus one dollar. Larry had the same rights. It was a mutual deterrent. With the shotgun clause as part of the deal, Larry had to be very careful before trying to buy me out.

I went to Moe with a draft agreement, and he had only one condition – if Hy showed up with a deal at the last minute, he would have to sell to him. But for now we had a deal that Moe and I were happy with. I then approached Ralph and Larry with my plan, and they agreed to the deal because they felt they had no choice since the company could fail at any time.

Because Moe was guaranteeing the company's line of credit for the first two years, the bank told Larry and me to come up with $5,000 each and they'd loan us the balance needed to complete the deal. Luckily, I had a good credit history at the bank, thanks to some great advice from my wife, Sandra. She came from a business-oriented family who owned several retail stores called Herman Brothers. One day, soon after we got married, she said, "Why don't you borrow $5,000?" I replied that I didn't need $5,000, but she said, "Just do it to establish your credit profile at the bank. You never know when you'll need it." I borrowed $5,000 from the Montreal City and District Savings Bank and paid it all back in six months. So when I needed a loan to buy Peerless, they gave me $5,000 right away.

The day before we went to the lawyer's office, Larry and I had an argument, the first of many. Peerless hadn't closed its financial statement for the prior year and the biggest part of valuing the company in the deal was going to be the pricing of the inventory on that financial statement. It was my first real lesson in the importance of valuing inventory in determining the value of a company. Moe had told us, "You come up with the number." Larry, Ralph, and I walked through the warehouse and we started arguing – which was a definite sign of things to come. Larry had bought the fabric at four dollars a yard. I said, "Larry, it's now worth three dollars." "No," he said, "I'm a great buyer; it's actually worth five dollars." I was trying to price the inventory at a fair market value but Larry, allowing his ego to get in the way, did not realize that the higher we priced the inventory, the more we'd have to pay for the company. Ralph didn't get involved in the pricing because he felt he had a conflict of interest with his brothers. I didn't fight too hard because I wanted the deal to pass, and I knew Peerless would be a great success going forward. We finally agreed on the price of the company and included ten years of a consultant's salary for Moe Segal in the deal.

Moe's guarantee with the bank really made the deal possible; that's how badly he wanted to get out. The day we drove to the lawyer's office to sign, I was very nervous. I kept picturing Hy Segal showing up at the last minute with the deal that had eluded him for almost four years. He never showed up, and we signed the papers. At twenty-six years of age, I was now a twenty-five-per-cent partner in Peerless Clothing. I kept my job, only now I would be called "vice president of manufacturing."

5

Be Careful, I Have a Shotgun!

After we made the deal and bought Peerless Clothing from Moe, Hy Segal walked out of the company and didn't speak to his brother or me for the rest of his life. It divided the Segal family between those who sided with Moe and those who sided with Hy. Moe tried for years to repair things with his brother, but he was never forgiven for selling half the company to "outsiders." I guess I was considered an outsider.

From my perspective, I had nothing to lose in my new partnership. I had put together a good deal, and I felt very positive and comfortable. I was making $14,000 a year plus an annual $1,000 bonus. I loved my work, I loved the factory, and I was having a great time learning. Maybe I was naive, but it didn't seem like that big a risk to me. Because of the shotgun clause in my agreement with Larry, I felt I had a tremendous amount of authority and could guide the company in the proper direction. I also saw it as a tremendous challenge.

What was clear to me was that our partnership wouldn't be smooth sailing. We actually had a fight on the drive back from the lawyer's office! The ink wasn't even dry on the contract and Larry said he wanted to sell the company. He didn't understand the potential of the deal we had just made. I said, "Larry, you're crazy. We just bought the company – we're going to build something." "No," he said. "We should sell it and make some money." I said, "Moe travelled all over the country for almost four years and couldn't find someone to buy it. Who are *you* going to sell it to?" Larry seemed to think we'd priced the inventory low and made ourselves a good deal. That argument would continue all through the 1960s.

For nine years we fought over everything. We struggled and never made a profit. We survived because credit was very loose; interest rates were low and that helped us through the rough patches. Throughout the sixties, we didn't pay anything back on our loan other than the interest, which in those days we could deduct from our personal gross income at the end of each year. We were constantly trying to make a profit and improve things, but without success. We could never agree on anything, and the company's financial instability and the pressure it created aggravated our tenuous relationship.

With the tension increasing day after day, coming to work became almost unbearable. Larry blamed me for everything and I blamed him, while Ralph watched the accusations bounce back and forth like a surly tennis match. At one point, we called in our senior auditor to give us some advice on how to run the company profitably instead of just breaking even. His conclusion was that none of us was capable of running the business.

We just muddled through, day by day. I don't know why we had such a hard time making money. Maybe it was the competition or maybe we weren't showing the right product. We had the same problem at the end of every year: how do we value the inventory? I wanted to change the marketing and merchandising. I hardly knew what those words meant in those days, but I knew our product was as good as anything else being sold out there. It just needed to be priced properly and sold to the right customers. I pointed out that Larry was buying the wrong fabric and paying too much for it, but I was a minority partner so nothing changed.

One of the first things I did when I became a minority partner was to put in the piecework incentive system that I had long ago wanted for the factory. (I never told Moe about it.) To achieve this, I needed an engineer who understood the system. KSA, the consultants I'd been using off and on at every opportunity to improve the factory's efficiency, introduced me to Ernie Siesel, a fellow who was running a very efficient shirt factory near Atlanta,

Georgia. Ernie was a manager and an engineer and exactly what I was looking for. I went to Atlanta to visit the factory and made a deal with Ernie to come to Montreal and be my plant manager.

Ernie and I worked together very closely on improvements to the factory and production methods, and I thought we were making good progress. However, Ralph and Larry never accepted him, and every year when bonus time came I'd end up fighting with them about Ernie's value to the company. Ernie felt it wasn't a good environment for him so, much to my disappointment, he left after five years, after only partially installing the incentive system. While in Montreal, Ernie met a lovely lady named Pierrette, and when they married I was at their wedding.

In spite of the continuous battles with Larry and Ralph, I was still able to improve and develop the factory with the latest equipment, technologies, and methods available during that period. Fortunately for us, Moe's guarantee on the Peerless line of credit meant I was able to make the necessary modifications to the factory, and, together with the government's depreciation incentive, we continued to modernize. I never allowed management turmoil to affect the factory's progress.

After two years Moe Segal was no longer involved in the business, but I kept him up to date on how things were progressing. I benefitted from his advice when things were tough at Peerless, but I knew he wanted to hear only the good things so that's exactly what I told him. I always appreciated the opportunity he'd given me when I turned eighteen, and our relationship continued to grow. He was really the only father I ever knew, and I felt that I needed him as a father figure for stability in my life, as well as for my wife and children. I stayed close with him for the rest of his life, and my stepsister Greta even remembers his mentioning me on his deathbed. He had made my first working years a pleasure, and I made sure to make the last years of his life comfortable.

One of the lowest points in my partnership with Larry and Ralph came in 1962. Our lease was up at 55 Pine Avenue East, and we needed more space. We had only 24,000 square feet and were crammed into our current location. Even though I suspected they wouldn't like it, I told them I wanted to move the factory

5.1 Moe Segal (left) and me (right), early 1970s

and the cutting room to one location in order to increase efficiency. Larry and Ralph said, "No. We can't afford it." Eventually I told them I had already signed a lease.

They were so upset that I had signed the lease that they tried to fire me. In those days, we had customer order pads with carbon paper and tissue in between. One day, we were in the showroom fighting and Ralph tore off a piece of tissue paper and wrote: "Don't come in tomorrow! You're fired!" He handed the note to me, and I said, "Ralph, you know what you can do with this tissue paper." I knew he couldn't fire me, and so did he.

Every time we fought, I'd say, "Make me an offer," but neither of them had the money to do that; I knew I was safe because of the shotgun clause in my agreement with Larry. Ralph knew about that clause, and he was terrified that one day I might buy out Larry and wind up owning fifty per cent of Peerless. For nine years, I used that clause for protection.

The lease I'd signed was with the Reichmann Brothers, the same family that went on to build the real estate giant Olympia and York, which developed Canary Wharf in London, England,

and the World Financial Center in New York. Under the name Three Star Construction, they were putting up a new building at 9600 St Laurent Boulevard. It was in the block next to our cutting room at 9500 St Laurent, and they needed a principal tenant in order to get financing.

Luckily for me, either they hadn't learned too much about real estate yet or they were desperate to get the project going. Either way, I was able to negotiate a great deal. I signed a twenty-five-year lease for a whole floor, approximately 60,000 square feet, at one dollar per square foot with only a "cost of living" escalation. I told Edward Reichmann, the oldest brother, who I was dealing with, that I needed steam for my presses and asked, "What are you going to charge me for steam?" He said, "I don't know – mark down the market rate." So I did. In those days, the price of oil was less than five dollars a barrel. Neither of us had any idea how that lease would affect us both in the future.

By the time the new building was finished, I knew we had a terrific lease, and I went ahead, hired a truck, and moved everything over a long weekend. We needed more space in the factory, and I wanted to reunite everything under one roof. I knew the factory was the key to Peerless and that the shipping room and the cutting room had to be attached to it. I even designed nice offices for Larry and Ralph, so they had nothing to complain about. Around the same time that we moved into the new premises, my son, Joel, was born.

As inflation kicked in and hit the oil market, Three Star Construction realized they were losing money on the building because they couldn't increase the price of steam. Edward Reichmann, with whom I'd been dealing on our lease, made *aliyah* to Israel about that time. His brothers may have encouraged him to do so, because right afterward they sold the property. The new owners didn't do their due diligence when they purchased the building, and soon sold it. Once more, we had a new landlord. When he realized how much our steam was costing him, he turned it off, saying, "I'll turn on the steam when a judge tells me to." We immediately took out an injunction, and within twenty-four hours the judge ruled in our favour, telling the new owner that Peerless's

5.2 In 1962, my business partners and I, along with our wives, celebrated Peerless's move to our new building at 9600 St Laurent Boulevard. Left to right, back row: Ralph Segal, Larry Lovell, me. In front: our wives Barbara Segal, Bernice Lovell, and Sandra Segal.

employees had to keep working, and he had to turn the steam back on. The building was not profitable for the owners until our twenty-five-year lease expired in 1987.

Meanwhile, Peerless went along as it had before with half of our working day spent fighting. One day, it got so bad that Larry threw a pair of scissors at me. I ducked, and the scissors tore a hole in the canvas of a painting behind me. Larry complained that Moe had charged us too much for the company. I said, "Larry, Moe left it to us to value the inventory, which affected the price we paid for the company, so don't complain if we priced it too high."

All Larry wanted to do was sell the company. At one point, Larry and Ralph brought in a representative from the well-known, publicly owned American suit manufacturer Hart Schaffner Marx, which was interested in buying other suit manufacturers. I was called to the meeting where the potential buyer asked each of us why we wanted to sell. He asked Ralph, who answered, "I want to move to Israel." He asked Larry, who said, "I want to make some money." Then he came to me and asked, "Alvin, why do you want to sell?" I said, "I don't want to sell! I want to build this company." He immediately stood up and said, while walking to the door, "If you'd all given the same answer as Alvin, I might have been interested!" Then he left. A lesson I learned from that meeting was that a clothing company without good management has nothing to sell. Management is everything. That's why Moe Segal wanted to sell the company in the first place.

For the nine years that Ralph, Larry, and I were partners, we often argued about what would happen if someone died. Ralph and Larry were both obsessed with the idea of getting insurance in case a partner passed away, maintaining that if you had one million dollars in insurance the company was worth two million dollars. I knew that calculation was wrong, that the insurance doesn't go to the bottom line; it would just help you buy out your partner's estate. It was one more argument we could never settle, so we never took out insurance.

Ralph owned half the business and ran the office. Larry bought the fabric and sold the suits. I ran the factory. Because I was convinced Larry wasn't buying the right fabrics, wasn't selling at the right price, and didn't know how to put the line together, we kept on arguing. Larry insisted that we weren't making money because the factory costs were too high, but if I had learned anything, it was how to keep costs down. One day, Ralph would say, "Alvin's right," and the next day he'd say, "Larry's right."

It should never have been so complicated. Men's clothing isn't really advanced fashion; the basic men's suit has not changed much in the past half-century. Men's wear is not like ladies' wear, where fashion and style dictates a whole range of changes every season. In men's wear, from one year to the next, the lapel might be an eighth of an inch or a quarter-inch wider or narrower, the coat might be half an inch longer or shorter, but a blazer is a blazer. Fabrics haven't changed that much either; a black wool suit is a black wool suit. It's basically a stable business, and the rest comes down to quality, price, and customer service.

In the late sixties, I was still working towards implementing the incentive system in the factory. I tried changing the employees' salaries from an hourly rate to one based on piecework, which would allow operators to make more money through greater efficiency. I hired a new engineer to replace Ernie. I thought he was experienced and gave him full authority to put the system in place, but he went too far too fast. Instead of selling the operators on the new production and pay rate by explaining to them how they could benefit from it, he tried to force them to adopt it by threatening them.

One day, I came back to work after lunch, and, to my surprise, found a sit-down strike going on in our coat factory. All the operators sat at their machines with their hands folded and refused to work. I went onto the factory floor and asked a few operators, "Why aren't you working?" They told me that they were afraid to work because they were being threatened. They led me to one of our lining pressers, Guy, who seemed to be leading the sit-down situation. I knew Guy very well, and he quickly told me that if I fired the new engineer they would all go back to work. He said that the new engineer had threatened the employees, telling them they would get fired if they didn't achieve the new production rates. I told Guy, "Tell the people to go back to work now, and I will deal with the situation at the end of the day." I couldn't let Guy get the best of me and be in control of the factory. Either he was in charge or I was! He didn't budge, so I said, "Then let everyone leave." I guess I don't like people to threaten me with ultimatums. Certainly, at that moment, I knew the incentive system was the right thing for the long-term success of our factory.

As everyone got up from their machines and punched out, I stood at the punch clock, took each one's card and said, "I'm very sorry you're leaving, but I can't let anyone control my factory; you're fired." As they were leaving, I realized that they were departing by ethnic groups – the French left together, the Italians left together, and so on. All of a sudden, the line stopped punching out, and only the Greek people were left. They said, "Mr Segal, we don't want to leave, but we are afraid." At that moment, someone told me that everybody who had just punched out was waiting in the lobby downstairs at the entrance of the building. I went down to meet them and, after listening to them, realized no one really wanted to leave. So I agreed to let them return to work the next morning without penalty.

At the end of that day, as things calmed down, I met with the engineer and had to fire him. He had no right to threaten employees. Selling incentive rates to employees requires patience and delicacy; they can't be forced onto workers. I had just learned another valuable lesson: If you put somebody in charge, make sure you follow up to ensure that the person is doing the job properly. I never wanted to give my employees a reason to go to the union and shouldn't have given the engineer full authority to put the incentive system in place.

I was worried about who would come back the next morning. Most of the factory employees returned the next day. About forty, however, had signed cards to join the Amalgamated union. I offered to let them return to the factory with everyone else, but the union told them to picket in front of the building instead of taking my offer. We hired security guards to stand at the door and make sure there was no trouble for employees crossing the picket line. It was the fall season, and the picketers continued their protest for about two months until the snow and cold weather drove them away.

Fortunately, the employees who decided to stand outside and protest were the high-priced earners, who would have been very difficult to put on the new incentive plan anyway. The union had made a major mistake: they should have allowed those employees to accept my offer to return to work because it would have been much easier to organize the factory from within. I trained new apprentices to replace the jobs left vacant. We had to lower production for a short time but ended up saving money in the long run.

A new leader emerged in the factory. Mariette Wylie, a long-standing Peerless employee and one of our best operators, was very annoyed that some of her close friends had joined the

5.3 Amalgamated union members picket our factory following a sit-down strike over our piecework incentive program, 1968.

Amalgamated union. Many of her family members worked in the factory. In fact, when one of her grandparents passed away, we had to close the production line because so many members of her family (all operators) were at the funeral. She was very worried that if the Amalgamated union organized Peerless, our employees would lose the extra benefits they had, and that would have a great impact on her family and friends. To protect against that, Mariette began to organize an independent union for Peerless factory workers. With the help of a few lawyers, she formed a bonafide legal in-house union, managed by the Peerless factory workers: La Fraternité des Travailleurs de Vêtement pour Hommes, known as "La Fraternité," which was never recognized by UNITE.

We had to negotiate a new contract with Mariette and her team. Mariette became the president of the new in-house union and ran it for almost thirty years. During those years, she was appointed to the Joint Committee representing Peerless employees and all other independent factories until she retired. Mariette was an amazing politician and visionary, able to be on the side of the employees and on my side at the same time (although she was tough and didn't make it easy for me). Mariette, her team, and I worked together toward building the most efficient factory in Canada, with the employees benefiting from higher earnings. With her vision, the employees understood that if the factory kept up to date and was efficient, they would prosper along with the company. Many of those employees – including some of the younger members of Mariette's family – are still with us today.

Back then our customer service was terrible. Although I was in charge of the factory, I wanted to be put in charge of the shipping room as well in order to improve things. However, the shipping room was Larry's territory and Larry didn't know how to improve things. Ralph didn't either. I always believed that the shipping room should be an extension of the factory since they work hand in hand together on operations and scheduling. I believed that we should change and wrote a memo outlining some recommendations:

MANUFACTURING – A well-defined plan for improving our garments: both pants and coats. A definite scheduling of additional labour costs for production of a better garment and maintenance of a uniform standard. It must be obvious to all that our quality must improve if sales are to increase. How much quality and how fast must be clearly defined.

CONTROL – At present I believe this to be our biggest and most serious problem. We paid a substantial amount of money to Kurt Salmon Associates for a long-range program, involving more adequate systems, needed to manage our business. I would like to know why this entire program was shelved. Our business cannot grow unless we have proper information regarding sales, salesmen, credits, cloth purchased and delivered, profits on individual sales by cloth, cost of our inventory.

We discuss these problems every time we sit down in a ridiculous and Mickey Mouse manner and cannot come to any decisions because we do not have the proper facts. We cannot make proper judgments and decisions with the information we have today.

I also had a point to make about quality. Quality can mean many things: it can mean a bad fit, threads hanging from the garment, or a poorly packed suit that the customer blames on quality. It can also mean inferior fabric. The word "quality" is all-encompassing. There were so many things wrong with the way we were doing business then, and many things had to change, but there was only so much I could control from the factory.

In that same memo, I outlined my main recommendations for sales: "Without the proper control and precise information at his fingertips, I believe Larry's effectiveness is greatly hampered." I suggested that a program of management controls be implemented and that I be responsible for putting them in place. "I believe that, with my knowledge of manufacturing, I am best suited to do this work." I felt that if Larry was in operations, I could control him from the factory and suggested that he be named operations manager and Ralph sales manager. This would also have brought some structure to the company. Nothing came of it.

In 1951, when I joined the company, annual sales were two million dollars. By the sixties, with inflation and rising prices, sales increased to four or five million. The Quebec government kept raising the minimum wage and all wages followed. When I started there were no importations of finished suits, but by the mid-sixties, imports had started coming in, manufacturing started to go global, and competition was fierce. We couldn't turn a profit.

At one point, in an attempt to get more sales and keep our salesmen from leaving because they weren't making enough commission, Larry raised the commission rate from the industry norm of five per cent to seven per cent. I said, "Larry, it won't raise our sales, but it will increase our losses, and it could put us out of line with the competition." He did it anyway.

Every year one of the three of us would buy a new car paid for by the company. At the end of 1968 it was my turn, but I suggested skipping a year because I knew the company couldn't afford it. Larry said that if I didn't buy a car he'd take my turn. I ended up buying a nice new Pontiac and drove it off the lot feeling terribly guilty. I knew the company could fail at any time.

There was always the thought in my mind of a creditor forcing us into bankruptcy. If we failed, how could I wind up with the factory and build a new company for the future?

Our situation got so bad that in January of 1969, Ralph called me into the office and said, "Alvin, we can't meet the payroll." We paid our employees on Thursdays, and he asked me to do whatever I could to buy some time. He said, "Stop the factory, and we'll issue the cheques Monday so we can gain the interest float over the weekend." Interest rates were high enough back then that just keeping the money in the bank for another four days would be worth it. Also, a couple of extra days for the collection of receivables would benefit us. On Thursday morning, payday, I pulled a fuse in the compressor to stop the factory and sent everyone home. Nobody knew the real story, and we were able to issue the cheques on Monday.

That's how close we were to the brink. We were so late on our payables that any supplier could have put us out of business. Things couldn't get worse, and no one had the answer on how to fix them. In the back of my mind, I was always thinking about different options and scenarios that might enable me to save the company.

6

I Have a Long-Range Plan
That Changes Every Day

In February 1969, I had the opportunity to take a ten-day vacation to Israel. It was two years after the Six Day War, and there was euphoria in the Jewish world. People were proud of Israel's success and the growing economic prosperity in the country. I had wanted to visit Israel since 1948 when I was fourteen years old, sitting beside the radio with my mother in Albany, listening to the United Nations vote on the creation of the State of Israel. Now, after years of learning about Israel whenever I could, soaking up Jewish history, I was finally getting the chance to visit. My wife Sandra didn't want to go because she and her family thought the region was still too dangerous, but I wanted to forge a deeper connection with my Judaism during what was a crucial time in Israel's young history. I decided to join a tour group out of New York and went on my own.

The tour went to Jerusalem, Tel Aviv, and other parts of the country. I was the youngest person in the group. When we went to Masada, I ran up the mountain ahead of everyone, took a run around the top, saw a bunch of stones, rocks, holes in the ground and little excavations, and I thought I'd seen everything. On my way down, I met the group still walking on their way up and told the guide I was done and would wait for them to finish. The guide, who was phenomenal, said, "But you don't know the story!" I spent the next couple of hours hearing about how Jewish rebels fended off the Roman soldiers and then perished rather than succumb to them. When the story was over, I had goose bumps.

6.1 On a hilltop overlooking Jerusalem during my first trip to Israel, 1969.

My Jewish identity, which I didn't really understand until I arrived in Israel, exploded on that trip. I was thirty-five and finally getting in touch with my Jewish roots. It was the experience of a lifetime.

After that break from the company and its problems, I returned to Montreal and found out that Ralph Segal had also left town, on a ski trip to Denver, Colorado. While on the ski slopes he'd suffered a heart attack and was taken to the hospital. A few days later, he passed away. The enormous pressure he'd been under must have taken its toll; Ralph was only forty years old. It was a tragedy that shocked the entire Montreal Jewish community. My world was about to change all over again.

At that point, things were very bad at Peerless. The years of fighting and mismanagement had caught up with us, and the company was a hair's breadth away from going out of business. The stress of that reality and the fact that we didn't know how to fix it had probably aggravated Ralph's heart condition and diabetes. After his death, I went through his desk at work and discovered a drawer full of pills. Ralph had obviously been suffering long before his trip to Denver, but he had never shared that with anyone.

Ralph was gone, and now I had Larry Lovell as my only partner, and on paper we were bankrupt. Within twenty-four hours of Ralph's death, in walked our auditor who knew the state of the company. He told us he was the trustee of Ralph's estate and he was going to buy us out and wind up the company. Based on the facts this was the practical thing to do, but I was extremely angry, and he had no idea what was going on in my mind. I turned to him and said, "Fuck you. We're buying the estate out." He turned around and left. As soon as the auditor walked out of the room, Larry asked me furiously, "How are we going to buy the estate out?" I completely lost my cool. "If you don't like it," I snapped, "I'll buy you out too!"

Everything was happening so fast, and I was so angry I don't know what came over me: I had no plan whatsoever. My reaction was totally impulsive, and I just went with my gut instinct. I had been ready to save the company before Ralph's passing and this tragedy hadn't changed my mind. Yes, Ralph's death had shocked me, but I was prepared to do everything in my power to keep my job and keep the factory going. I was convinced that I could control the destiny of Peerless because I knew the product so well, down to every last detail of every operation. Starting in the factory at eighteen years old had clearly given me an advantage over my partners.

The next day, the auditor came back and agreed that the estate would sell their shares; it was as simple as that. We didn't set the price right away. To me the value of the company was still one million dollars, the same as it had been when we'd bought it from Moe Segal almost a decade earlier. The estate's share was around $500,000. Arguing with Larry about how to buy out the estate, with or without him, went on for several months. We couldn't agree on a deal for the same reasons we couldn't operate as partners throughout the sixties. That partnership just wasn't meant to be.

Buying out the estate would ensure that Ralph's family would have enough money to continue their way of life. I had lost my own father at a young age, and although Ralph's children were a little older than I had been when my father died, I felt responsible for Ralph's family and how his estate would be looked after. Ralph's wife, Barbara, thanked me for making sure her interests were taken care of in the transition. To achieve that, I knew the company had to be completely reorganized, but I was still just an inside man running the factory and was in no position to take it over all by myself. I had to figure out what to do. The company had to keep operating and I had to keep Peerless's legacy going.

The solution came in the form of an offer I received from my sister's father-in-law, Moe Lazare, which occurred even before Ralph was buried. In fact, Ralph's autopsy and funeral took well over a week because his body had to be transported from Colorado to Montreal. I was spending Passover weekend in Florida when I happened to meet Moe while walking on the beach. It was right after Ralph's passing, and Moe asked me, "Is there any chance I could be your partner?" I knew Moe Lazare through the family and from Elm Ridge, but he knew nothing about the garment industry. Although his offer to be my business partner was a great compliment, I wasn't convinced it was a good idea and needed time to think it over.

His daughter had just married Otto Sand, who had been part of our crowd when I met my wife Sandra, and Moe Lazare wanted to get him involved in a business. Otto had previously been a salesman for a men's shirt company. I liked him and thought he knew the industry and might be what I needed for the outside of my business.

When I returned to Montreal, I discussed Moe Lazare's offer with my friend, lawyer, and confidant Nahum Gelber. He had been my next-door neighbour when we moved to Isabella Avenue in 1950 and we'd stayed close friends ever since. During our conversation, he admitted that he would like to be my business partner and said, "Don't go with the Lazares. I'll give you sixty per cent of the company, and I'll take forty per cent. I like the way you operate and I'd love to be your silent partner." I had no vision of owning Peerless alone or any ambition to be president. I just wanted to keep the company running as I always had and felt that to achieve that goal I would need an active partner to run the outside of the business. Nahum Gelber's offer to be my silent partner wasn't what I thought I needed at that time. If only I had taken his offer into consideration a lot of the turmoil to come would have been avoided.

The tension in the company had been building long before Ralph died but now it got worse, with some key people in the office and shipping siding either with Larry or with me. The controller, who had sided with Ralph when he was alive, was now on Larry's side. This was the same woman who, before I had left for Israel, had handed me one hundred dollars from petty cash with an ominous, "I hope the plane crashes." She'd be the first to go if I ever took control of the company. Another person with whom I had always fought head to head was Larry's right hand and shipping room manager, Charlie Macfarlane. To Larry's delight, Charlie would take every opportunity to disagree with me. Charlie was convinced that if I ever got control of the company, he'd be the first one I would let go. (In fact, once I had control of the company Charlie stayed with me until he retired, working inside sales and eventually taking over the Ottawa territory as a commissioned salesman.) Except for Larry and Ralph and those few people who were closely allied with them, everyone in the company liked me and knew what I wanted to achieve if we were able to continue in business.

Taking over the company was constantly on my mind, but I didn't believe that I could run the business on my own. At that moment, I sincerely felt I needed a partner who knew the outside of the business. For that reason, I went with Moe's offer and not with Nahum Gelber's. I needed Moe's money, his guarantee at the bank and, mainly, his son-in-law to replace Larry in sales and merchandising. Moe didn't even ask for a contract. As far as I know, he didn't know the condition of the company nor did he seem to care. Apparently, he and his family had a lot of confidence in me. Had they done their due diligence, they might have had second thoughts. In the end, we settled the deal on a handshake. I would be running the company, and Larry would finally be out of my life.

Although I had Moe Lazare's backing, I still had to make a deal with Ralph's estate. In one of our discussions, Larry said to me, "I have somebody to support me. I'm going to make a deal with the estate, and I'll buy you out." At another time, he sent me a telegram: "I am opposed to the purchase, by you, of any of the estate shares, at any time, without my consent and I will hold you responsible for all damages resulting from your failure to abide by our shotgun agreement, and will attack any transaction, made by you or the estate, in breach of my rights." For about a year it was like the Wild West. Anything could have happened to the company during that period.

Peerless had capital from the Segal family in the form of demand loans. I knew that anyone buying Peerless would have to support the banking arrangements and replace those loans. I went to a few relatives and friends and asked if they wanted to invest in the company that I was going to buy. To my surprise, I had people willing to support me.

Now, if Larry wanted to buy me out, he had to replace those loans as well as buy out Ralph's estate, and I knew he couldn't manage that. Moe Lazare had made the offer to me alone, and Larry was never part of the deal. Looking back, I don't think Larry ever realized that I could get the money and the partners together to obtain full control of the company and get rid of him.

One day I got a call from Bill Alexander at the TD bank. He said, "Alvin, I've never met you, but your partner was just here and he wants to buy you out. Can you come down to the bank? I'd like to meet you." I didn't know Bill, but I went to meet him. After talking with me for about ten minutes, he said, "I think you should buy Mr Lovell out. I'll support you." To this day, I have no idea how or why this happened, but I've always wondered if Bill had heard from our auditor, Marvin Corber, that I was a better risk than Larry. Thankfully, in those days a manager at the local branch had a lot more authority than they do today. He didn't need approval from head office to make a decision like that.

Talking to Bill gave me the confidence to buy out Larry once and for all. I introduced the Lazares to Bill Alexander, and, with the Lazares' guarantee, we were able to restructure Peerless. Going forward it would be almost like a new company. We bought Larry's shares and Ralph's estate, paying Larry $300,000 for his share of the company – $50,000 more than it was worth – just to settle the deal. On his way out the door Larry told me, "You're going to fail, because you don't know the customers." As it turned out, it was the other way around: Larry put all his money into a company called Cornwall Pants, which didn't last more than a year.

Our biggest customer was Sears catalogue, and Larry had predicted I'd lose them because I didn't know any of their buyers. The day after Larry left, I got a call from Sears. "Alvin, we hope you're still going to sell to us. We need you." It was soon very clear that our customers weren't going to leave, and I discovered what a good salesman I was, even with my stutter, as I started dealing directly with them. Now, as president, although I had not planned to do so, along with running the factory I became the outside person responsible for sales, inventory, and fabric-buying. I was running the whole business.

With this change the Lazare family and I each owned fifty per cent of Peerless, with the understanding that I would be president and have the controlling vote. We had nothing in writing and didn't discuss a plan for the future. We didn't sit down and talk about the specifics; Moe simply put the money down and signed at the bank. He was just happy that Otto would be working with me.

I was confident that I could turn the company around. I knew nothing about sales or customer service or any of the other areas of the company that clearly needed fixing, but I was so comfortable running the factory that I felt I had nothing to lose, and I'd figure it out. I knew we just had to get the right fabric, cut it, sew it, keep shipping, and collect receivables. I just had to keep the factory running and thought Otto would handle the outside of the business.

On 4 March 1970, after working at Peerless for almost nineteen years, I took over as president. Ralph and Larry were gone, and I was in charge of everything, with all the responsibility on me. Everything had happened so fast, but at that moment, I felt so relieved that I decided to focus only on the future. I called a meeting in order to introduce my new partner, Otto Sand, to the staff. I let them know that he would run the outside sales and that I would run the inside operations and manufacturing. I was so excited that my stutter became worse, and I had great difficulty introducing him.

I wanted to avoid potential problems in the future by limiting the Lazares' involvement in the business to Otto only. I didn't want any other members of his family in the business. Moe agreed. Unfortunately, it became apparent to me very soon that Otto had neither the experience nor the retail contacts in the men's suit industry required to be successful in his new position. He knew nothing about the tailored suit industry, including the product and the fabrics used. What did I expect? How can somebody who knows nothing about a product successfully sell it to clients? The poor guy was destined for failure. I quickly realized he couldn't possibly provide the help I needed for the outside of the business. Had I made a mistake?

I soon learned that I had totally underestimated what it meant to run a company. Now that I was in charge of all decision-making, I could no longer criticize from the sidelines. Not only did I have to teach Otto who our suit buyers and textile mill contacts were, I had to fix all the things that weren't working and that was just about everything except for the factory. For the previous decade, I had been isolated from some of Peerless's biggest problems since Ralph and Larry were running their areas, even if they were running them badly. Now I had to make the decisions and deal with the consequences myself. I was basically building a new company on the bones of the old one, and, unfortunately, I started to neglect the factory.

During those years, I had been buying the trimmings for men's jackets: pocketing, linings, and shoulder pads, etc. One of the things I needed to improve immediately was the purchasing and scheduling of our shell fabrics (the outside material). During the late 1960s, we started moving away from synthetic fabrics and into wool. I knew from my experience in the factory that some of the fabric Larry had been buying didn't tailor properly. All I really knew about the shell fabric was how it was tailored into a finished product; in the factory you knew which materials were easy to handle.

Why hadn't we been making money all those years? The factory was as good as any in the business. The problem was not our production but the shell fabrics we were using. I had to make some immediate changes.

I contacted the president of Cleyn and Tinker, the local mill where we bought most of our fabric, and asked him to teach me about the different textiles they offered. I had to learn the technical distinction between the fabrics in order to know which ones we should and should not buy. I was able to pay much more attention to buying, but since it was a full-time job, I eventually hired a professional fabric-buyer named Ian Deakin.

Back in 1968, in preparation for the company's fiftieth anniversary in 1969, Ralph and Larry had introduced a big sales promotion: "Suits for fifty dollars." I was against it because we would lose money at that price, but they went ahead and bought the fabric anyway. In their anticipation of this event being such a great success, they had ordered enough fabric to keep the factory going for at least a year. Unfortunately, the sales never happened and we ended up owning so much inventory that we didn't buy any more fabric for another season.

This led directly to one of the smartest decisions I made at the start of my new partnership with the Lazares. Through our agreement we had restructured the company, essentially creating a new one, and the bank didn't care about the books for the previous season. That meant I could close the previous year at a substantial loss by reducing the value of the entire fabric inventory. I knew I'd be able to sell all the suits made from that fabric and make a profit going forward. As it turned out, I started showing a profit the first year the Lazares and I were in business because I valued the fabric so low.

One of the lessons I had learned during the purchase of Peerless ten years earlier was the importance of valuing inventory. The value of the total inventory – fabric, work in process, finished garments, trimmings, etc. – at year-end is the value of the company for that moment in time. So, if you value the inventory low at the end of the year (and thereby defer profits), you have an opportunity to make a profit going forward. If you value the inventory high, you show a profit for that year but have nothing in reserve for the next year. I've always taken the conservative route and valued the previous year's inventory as low as I can and still have the auditor sign the company statement. Another manufacturer once told me that at the end of the year, "It's not what your sales are; it's the total inventory you're left with that really counts." At the end of the year, I'm a pessimist looking back in order to be an optimist looking forward.

In the 1960s, before we had computers, we had no idea of our year-end results until the auditor's report came in three months later. There were no management information systems in those days, just the accountant who came in around Christmas to review our results. Larry, Ralph, and I would have a dollar betting-pool amongst ourselves, guessing how Peerless had done that last year. I was always closest to the actual number.

I knew that one of the challenges in our factory was late delivery. We were buying our fabrics too late, and that caused delays with the cutting and sewing. All of our production was rushed; we had rush orders on top of rush orders, and it made me crazy. I realized that having an earlier year-end would force us to buy our fabric and show our line sooner, which would make our factory more efficient. It would also bring us more in line with the retail calendar. Every retailer knows that he doesn't want fall goods after the end of September and doesn't want spring goods after the end of March. After taking over, I changed our year-end from 30 November to 30 September. We started thinking like retailers, and to this day the company operates on a 30 September year-end. This had a lot of positive side effects, including fewer rush orders, no more delays in production, fewer overtime hours, and more flexibility.

I then focused on improving my management team. I hired Ben Lipes from Daymor Pants, in December 1970, to run the odd pants business (a separate business making and selling trousers only, no jackets), because when you're making suits, you need a separate trouser business to keep the pants factory running. Here's how Ben remembers his arrival at the company:

> Ian Deakin had mentioned me to Alvin. He contacted me
> at Daymor Pants. I met Alvin and Otto; the story was that
> Otto was in charge of sales and was Alvin's partner. It was a
> Saturday morning, Alvin showed me the office, and he didn't
> have a key so he climbed over the top of a partition. That was
> my first introduction to Alvin Segal – nothing is going to stop
> him. He said he needed somebody to run the odd pants com-
> pany and separate it from the suit business. I told him I had
> never run a pants company. He said, "Don't worry, I'll be
> there." I said that I couldn't do sales. He said, "Don't worry,
> we have the sales." I said, "Then, what do you need me for?"
> and he told me, "We need somebody to coordinate it."

Ben helped me organize our production scheduling; he knew the industry and understood how to respond to the changes that were happening. He and I became close, and he was doing so well on the pants side that I began pulling him into suits to work with me. After a few months, I decided that we didn't need a fabric buyer because Ben could do that too. Eventually Ian Deakin left, and Ben and I took over the buying. I liked the direction we were taking, so when I phased out of the buying, Ben took over while continuing to manage the odd pants business.

The apparel business was changing fast as new styles and trends emerged, including leisure suits. At our 1971 fall sales meeting, I summed it up:

> This past season has seen the greatest change in the men's
> clothing market ever. All over the United States and Canada,
> manufacturers have been trying to meet past season's figures
> and have not done so. Some large firms have closed their
> doors because they could not cope with the new markets,
> double knit fabrics, styles, and methods. Everyday problems
> notwithstanding, we must be doing something right with

young aggressive management and sales personnel in probably the most flexible men's clothing operation in Canada. The single factor contributing most to our success and flexibility is our ability to make changes in the factory at any moment and not be held back by the sectoral union. Also, the shift in consumer demand to more popular priced clothing helped, as we are here to meet this demand. We intend to stay with it – keeping our reputation as Canada's best value in clothing and of course, keeping in mind the style explosion of double-knit fabric prevalent today.

Slowly but surely, things were moving in the right direction. I was learning more about the business beyond the factory because I had no choice. Looking back today, I realize how foolish I had been to think that taking over the company would be smooth sailing. But it forced me to become immersed in areas I never would have learned about otherwise, and that definitely made me a better president.

7

Building a Management Team

By the end of 1970 I'd been president for less than a year, and the changes I was making to the company were quickly producing results. Reducing the value of the fabric left over from our failed fiftieth-anniversary sale allowed me to set the price of our suits very low, and we started showing a profit right away. The Lazare family didn't understand what was going on; all they saw was a huge increase in our sales volume and our profits. I made it look easy, and they must have thought Peerless was the best dream investment they could ever have hoped for.

In the meantime I was very unhappy, because I wasn't getting the support I needed to run the company and was running it without their help. I was spending so much time managing the outside of the business – sales, merchandising, and administration – that the factory was being neglected, and the downsides of my deal with the Lazares were beginning to seriously outweigh the benefits. Very early in our partnership, I realised I'd made a mistake going with the Lazares. It hadn't been fair to expect Otto to run the outside of the business; we had set him up for failure. I felt I had to find a way out of our partnership. I could run the company without the Lazares, but I needed to find new partners to be my management team.

I decided to bring Ernie Siesel back to run the factory. Ernie had been a factory engineer and my right-hand man at Peerless when I was still with Ralph and Larry. They hadn't appreciated him, and Ernie had felt pressured to leave and found another job. He was now working for a company called Mr Sport, where he wanted to stay because he was about to become a junior partner. Without consulting with the Lazares I told Ernie, "I can offer you a partnership at Peerless," and I offered him ten per cent of the business. I thought that since Otto hadn't worked out, Ernie's share would come out of the Lazares' half of the company, but they replied, "No. We'll give up whatever you do, but we're not going to have fewer shares than you." That's when the tension began. This wasn't just about business; it also affected my family because my sister Harriet was married to Moe Lazare's son, Jack. My sister and I had always been very close. Our children were the same age and were friends and we would even plan family weekends and vacations together.

In hindsight, I'm glad the Lazares refused to accept my suggestion to sell ten per cent to Ernie because that would have made them silent partners, and in my opinion there is no room in this industry for silent partners. On the other hand, I wasn't about to give up anything because I felt that I was running the company myself, without any help from them. So I offered to buy back their shares and let them leave the partnership. They counter-offered with the same deal and, because we didn't have a partnership agreement in writing, I knew that could lead to trouble. In spite of our disagreement over the shares, I was able to get them to sign a contract retroactive to the day we had become partners. They saw that the company was making a profit, so they agreed to sign a contract that gave me the deciding vote and that bought me some time.

The Lazare family agreed that Otto hadn't worked out, so they replaced him as their representative in the company by having my brother-in-law, Jack Lazare, come into Peerless once a month to keep the family informed about what was going on. By that time, I had learned enough about sales and merchandising to put the right people in place for whatever I couldn't handle myself.

Even though I had signed a contract, I still couldn't make a deal for Ernie's ten per cent. Clearly, the Lazares weren't the right partners for me, but they wouldn't let me buy them out. Ernie was waiting for my answer so, to trigger a decision, I cut the Lazares' draw (their management salary) from the company. That brought us to a shareholders' meeting with our lawyers. It lasted about ten minutes. The Lazares' lawyer said that their draw from the company couldn't be cut. My lawyer, knowing that I had the casting vote, passed me a note that read: "Conflict of interest." I told the Lazares' lawyer that his clients had a conflict of interest and that he was out of order – the words stumbled out of my mouth with much difficulty. That immediately broke up the meeting.

Soon after, I offered the Lazares double what they had paid a year earlier for their half of the company; they still refused. They offered to buy me out and I refused. Over the year, they had seen that Peerless was a viable business, and they thought the company could run on its own. They had very little experience and didn't realize all the good things I was doing for the company. When partners cannot agree, the situation has to be brought to a head. The Lazares ended up filing a motion to wind up the company, which was the smart thing to do because it forced us to reach a solution.

After they filed the motion, we went to court. The day of the hearing, my brother-in-law Jack took the stand and told the judge that the Lazare family was able to run the company or find the right people for the job. After hearing Jack's testimony, I called for a recess during which I raised my offer to buy them out, and we struck a deal. I thought the cost of the fight was getting too high. It was causing a rift between my sister Harriet and me, so I paid the Lazares more than double what they'd put into the company. The bank supported me because it had been following my performance since I'd taken over as president and had confidence that I could run Peerless on my own; it had seen the financial statements and watched how I had turned the company around so quickly. The deal I made to buy out the Lazares was worth it; we never set foot in a courtroom again.

Although I had taken over the business, I still felt I wasn't producing the changes the company needed. I wasn't satisfied with my knowledge of merchandizing and sales. I had never needed to know how to source fabric, how to show swatches and show a line, or how to deal with salesmen. My competitors were travelling to Europe to find new fabrics and the best trimmings, and I needed to start going in that direction as well. It was a tremendous challenge. I was still in a learning mode and searching for ways to improve things. I tried every idea that came along – many of which didn't work – and I needed new partners to help me.

Ben was doing great as my right-hand man, and the business was growing. I was able to give Ernie ten per cent of the company and offered Ben the same. I would own eighty per cent of Peerless. Then, after less than two years at Peerless, at the age of thirty-five, Ben had a minor heart attack. As he says, "A minor heart attack is something that happens to other people. When it happens to you, it's not minor." Ben came back after a month of recuperation, but he wasn't the same. "I spent a lot of time during the day checking my pulse, because I wasn't sure how much longer I was going to be around," he says now, at seventy-eight years old. Although I depended on Ben as a sounding board for everything, I had to keep moving forward without him. I had no choice. I reacted the way I always have: I kept going.

Ernie joined the company with a ten-per-cent share and started worrying far too much about issues beyond the factory. Because he was a shareholder, he was concerned about sales and how we were running the outside of the company instead of focusing on the factory and doing his job. Soon afterwards, he was diagnosed with an angina condition, which didn't help his worrying or his role in the company. A year after he'd joined Peerless, I offered to pay him his share of the profits. He left in 1974 without any hard feelings. I took over his ten per cent of the company and then owned ninety per cent, with Ben owning ten per cent. Ernie, his wife Pierrette, and their children moved to Florida where they still live today. We are both in Boca during the winter, and we spend time together whenever the opportunity arises.

On 31 October 1974, Montreal experienced a firefighters' strike. The newspapers called this horrific incident "Le Weekend Rouge." The strike created great anxiety, as fires in the city burned without intervention from firefighters. That Saturday morning, someone threw a Molotov cocktail through the ground-floor window of our factory at 9600 St Laurent Boulevard. I got an emergency call and came to see what had happened. By the time I got there the fire had already been extinguished by our sprinkler system, but there was so much smoke you couldn't see your hand in front of your face.

An insurance adjuster was already there, so I showed him our insurance policy. He took one look and said, "Go to Florida; I'll take care of everything." He had read the clause that George Wall had put in our contract about fifteen years earlier: "Replacement new at policyholder's discretion." The fabric room was located on the same floor as the fire, and there was smoke damage throughout. We made a claim to include the damaged fabric and even some old fabric had to be replaced. The money the insurance company gave Peerless was enough to pay off most of the loans the company had accumulated with the bank over the previous fourteen years. The city held a hearing immediately after the incident, and I was asked to testify under oath that I had had nothing to do with the fire. They knew at once that I was innocent.

For many years I had tried various people in key positions in the company, but I felt I wasn't getting anywhere. So I brought in Kurt Salmon Associates to help me build a management team. They conducted a study and produced an organizational chart that cost the company $100,000. It showed that I was involved in every aspect of the business. I was micromanaging: buying fabric, selling suits, managing the factory, and purchasing machinery. "You don't know how to delegate and hold people accountable," they said. "And you don't know how to interview and find the right people." I said, "If I could find the right people I would hold them accountable. Help me." I asked them to do the interviewing for me. I sat in on the interviews, and they ended up hiring six MBAS. I even paid KSA to do the training. A month later, Ben and I realized the new situation was a disaster. KSA ended up firing five of the six hirees themselves, and then I fired KSA. The last guy stayed for a month, but then left too. As Ben recalls:

If there was a weakness Alvin had, it was that he found people to come into the company that he thought he could develop.

We hired people thinking they would take us to another level. He didn't tell them how great we were, he told them all the things that were wrong. The guy would think, "Peerless is in a lot of trouble. I better start fixing things" rather than being smart enough to think "Let's see what they're doing right before I start changing things." Eventually they would all fail.

To keep the business running, I leaned on Ben more and more. Every day we sat down and considered how we were going to keep operating. That was the crucial thing. I always knew that keeping the business going meant keeping the factory running, even if we didn't have the sales. It's better to take a low margin than close the factory, because the fixed overhead (rent, hydro, management, etc.) is always there whether or not the factory is running.

There was a need in the market for ladies' suits and blazers made of men's suiting fabric. We formed a division and started producing ladies' wear, but realized quickly that this business involved a totally different cycle of selling and required different sales personnel. The blazers and suits sold well, but it was very difficult for us to manufacture the garments in our own factory because the J C rules were different for women's wear. Our men's wear sales team didn't have the right contacts, and the sales cycle for ladies' garments is completely different from the men's wear cycle. We could have stayed with it, but the juice wasn't worth the squeeze. Even today I get suggestions to go into ladies' wear, but I'm reluctant to do it for all the reasons we learned when we tried it the first time.

The company was becoming more efficient. That's what we were focusing on because I knew that everything else would come together. Here's how Ben recalls that period:

Alvin was fearless. He was never afraid of anything, in business or otherwise. He would say he worried about his stutter. I stopped noticing Alvin's stutter because it never stopped him from doing anything. He always had the same approach when he wasn't sure about things: if he didn't know, he'd learn. To

Alvin's credit, even though I had a small share, he always treated me like a partner. He always shared information with me and allowed me to do what I thought was right. We were a manufacturing-oriented company. We sold what we could make, as opposed to making what we could sell.

When I came in we were just starting to get into computers. We had a monster room with an IBM, a big mainframe with three files that tried to talk to each other; people were putting in information but had no idea what to do with it. There was no control, nobody around to say whether the information was right or wrong. But Alvin insisted we were going to be on computers. His main strength is that he's like a GPS – here's where we're going, here's how we're going to get there. If something gets in the way, he doesn't spend ten minutes worrying about it. "Okay, that's not going to work, never mind that. We'll go another way, but just keep going."

During that period, I needed more expertise in sales and marketing. I remembered that back in the '60s, while attending a machinery show in the US, I had become friendly with the vice president of manufacturing of Brookfield Clothing in New York. In exchange for a bottle of Crown Royal, he would sneak me through the back door of the factory in Queens and show me all the new machines and systems they were using. Brookfield had the latest machinery, and I learned a lot from those expeditions. I could tell from walking through their factory that Brookfield ran its business the way that I wanted to run Peerless.

What I had seen during those visits stayed in the back of my mind. Their marketing and merchandising techniques helped the factory produce more efficiently. They had proper and advanced planning: they worked earlier in the season and they bought their fabrics ahead of time. They would also cut and sew much larger quantities, which made the factory more efficient and production smooth.

I knew the name of Herman Soifer, the owner of Brookfield Clothing, from a real estate investment Moe Segal had made with him twenty years earlier. I decided to call him, and introduced

7.1 At the men's wear show in Las Vegas with my mentor, Herman Soifer, early 1990s.

myself as the owner of Peerless Clothing in Canada; I complimented him and told him I admired the way he ran his company. I said I'd like to meet him in New York to see if we had anything in common. When I met him we hit it off right away. I told him I'd just taken over the company, and asked if he'd be my consultant and teach me how to run the outside of a men's suit manufacturer. He had no concerns about helping me because Peerless didn't sell to the US in those days so we weren't in direct competition with Brookfield. Herman became a great business advisor and also a personal mentor. For almost twenty years, until he passed away at the age of ninety-seven, we had something close to a father-son relationship. He definitely taught me how to run the outside of a men's suit manufacturing business.

Herman helped us by letting us attend his sales meetings. Twice a year I would go to New York with my team to see how Herman ran a sales meeting and showed a line. We learned a lot about merchandising and the basics of customer service. Most of all it underscored what I already knew from my experience running Peerless's factory: the less variety you produce, the better. Ben recalls:

> Our weakness was in merchandising and marketing. We didn't know where we were going or what we were doing. We'd end up with a huge line, with many fabrics and styles. There was too much variety and not enough strategy. One of the things we learned from Herman was to say, "This is our limit. This is what we can make, so this is what we are going to sell." We had to narrow down our line. Alvin believed this, and so we changed and it made us more efficient.

The way Herman handled his salesmen opened a whole new world to me: he was a sales and marketing genius. As good as I was at handling things on the inside, that's how good Herman was at handling the outside. He knew his customers, he had confidence in his product, and every season he had new ideas to present to his salesmen about how to approach their retailers. I spent two or three years gaining knowledge through observing him and his team, but the US market was much bigger than our Canadian market so I couldn't really do in Canada what Herman could do in the States. After a few years we stopped going to Herman's sales meetings, but I always stayed in touch with him.

From that point on, I kept bringing in new people with experience in sales and merchandizing. Things were getting better and better. I learned from everyone in order to get myself to a new level of experience. I believed a good president should be aware of every aspect of his company, so I tried to manage and keep an eye on every department the best I could. As I learned more, I continually set new goals for myself and Peerless and felt very positive about the future.

8

The Engineered Suit:
The Collar Is Everything

Our big breakthrough came in the late 1970s with the introduction of the engineered suit. At that time, Europe was where fabrics and styles originated. Going to Europe was like looking into a crystal ball to see the future: what we saw there would show up in our market the following season. I attended many European shows, mostly in Germany and France. Machinery suppliers, in the hope I'd become a customer, took me to men's clothing factories to show me how their machines worked. What I ended up seeing was how the engineered suit was manufactured.

The concept of the engineered suit originated in Europe after the war. A European factory-owner once told me that so many Jewish tailors had been lost in the Holocaust or had fled the continent that German manufacturers started experimenting with mechanization to make up for the lack of tailoring expertise. I don't know whether that's true or not, but by the early to mid-seventies, when I was taking trips to Europe several times a year, I discovered the German manufacturers were making beautiful suits that sold at higher price points, and they were doing it with less skilled tailoring. It was an approach to suit manufacturing that differed completely, from pattern making to assembly, from the way suits were made in North America.

I immediately saw that it would solve most of the problems we were dealing with in our factory.

Back when I was eighteen and pairing in collars on the factory floor, the first thing I learned about suit manufacturing was that if the collar doesn't hug the neck and sit properly on the shoulders, the suit doesn't fit well. Getting the collar to fit properly is the hardest thing to achieve on a suit. I used to rack my brain to figure out how to get the collar right. The engineered suit was the solution. It produced the perfect collar automatically through a revolutionary approach to suit manufacturing. Rather than adding the collar last – as is done in traditional suit tailoring – the engineered suit *started with the collar* and built the garment around it. This was done by means of a paper pattern that shaped the collar instead of having operators build the collar through tailoring and pressing. The collar is the foundation of the engineered garment.

There were other ways that the engineered suit would solve some of the problems we faced in our factory. In addition to poorly fitting collars, we dealt with puckering fronts and twisted sleeves and pant legs. On hot, muggy Montreal summer days, the humidity in the air often caused the suits to pucker and we'd have to close the factory. The advent of fusing, used in the engineered suit, eliminated puckering fronts.

I could visualize the future, and it made sense to me that before the turn of the twenty-first century all popular priced, off-the-rack men's suits sold in North America would be engineered. Imported suits made by Hugo Boss in Germany were already selling at a much higher price-point in the North American retail market. They were pioneers in the field, and made an engineered suit that looked so good it became the fashion icon of the era. If Peerless could make an engineered suit like Hugo Boss, we would change the retailers' perception that we produced only a low-end product.

I wanted to start making our suits that way as soon as possible. This meant I would have to change every single operation in our factory and introduce new machinery, and because Peerless didn't belong to the sectoral union, we were in a unique position to do that. All over North America, the Amalgamated union exerted enormous control in the men's fine clothing industry. Company owners had to modify their union contracts if they wanted to make major changes in their factories. Although they all saw the engineered suit as the wave of the future, they had to negotiate with the union before taking advantage of the new system.

We made the changes gradually and for a time set up two lines, one for our engineered suit and one for our regular product, in the same factory. However, over the fifteen years between 1975 and 1990, we slowly transitioned to producing only the engineered suit. It was complicated, but we were fortunate we could make the changes in our existing factory. Some of our competitors wanting to switch to engineered suits had to open brand new factories to get around the sectoral union's control.

At Peerless, every operator and foreman had to be retrained. This also required changes in job descriptions, and I had to convince operators and foremen that we were doing the right thing. It was a huge endeavour and required a change in mindset: how we made suits *and* how we sold them. Every machine and operation had to be changed, from the pattern-making to how the pieces were put together. North American designers weren't familiar with the engineered suit system, so for a couple of years European designers would come for a week twice a year to produce patterns and samples for the upcoming season. I learned a tremendous amount from them.

At one of our first sales meetings, our salesmen complained they couldn't sell the engineered suit. I had a sample made and showed it to the team, but they said, "That's not tailored clothing. There is no tailoring in it." They saw the engineered suit as a deskilled garment and had a mental block against it because it wasn't made the conventional way. Some salesmen even threatened to leave, but I knew they were wrong. Hugo Boss was proving that the engineered suit could be sold at a higher price point in the retail market. I stuck with my conviction, and none of our salesmen left.

My vision slowly caught on and, by the late 1970s, took the industry by storm. Every year, the American Men's Clothing Manufacturers Association (AMCMA) held an industry seminar in New York and one year, they chose the engineered suit as their theme. Peerless had the largest attendance at that meeting. I had invited all our major customers, and they were blown away. Samples of the engineered suit were shown at the seminar and everyone could see that, even without traditional tailoring operations, great results could be achieved. Our customers encouraged me to go forward with the development in our factory.

Some retailers, however, didn't like the engineered suit because it couldn't be altered in the same way as a traditional suit. Some saw this as a problem, so I tried to introduce them to European metric sizing. In Europe, the metric scale – smallest size to largest – comes with two sizes more than the Imperial scale, which results in fewer alterations. With the metric system, retailers could have lowered their costs by reducing their alteration departments. However, switching measurements required too many changes and the Canadian men's suit and apparel industry didn't understand the benefits. We never switched to metric sizing, but the retailers did accept our new product with Imperial sizing. Today most suits in the low to medium price bracket are made by the engineered system, and retailers have adjusted accordingly.

While I learned more about suit manufacturing in the seventies, I also learned more about textiles (the shell fabric) and trimmings (everything in a suit but the shell fabric). I grew increasingly frustrated that the Canadian men's suit industry could not grow and prosper because of the duties and tariffs imposed by the federal government, as demanded by the Canadian textile industry. In order to succeed, the men's suit industry needed access to raw materials not made in Canada. This was especially true if we were making engineered suits, because the major distinction from one suit to the next is the shell fabric and the trimming used inside the garment. When our salesmen show our line to retailers for the upcoming season, they mainly show fabric swatches. It became obvious to me that the challenge was to find and use fabrics that our competitors didn't have, but by the mid-eighties there was only one worsted-wool mill left in Canada, and their offerings were very limited. They did not produce finer yarns and had few colour and pattern choices.

Every suit manufacturer, including me, travelled the world in hopes of finding something new: a textile that would differentiate us from our competitors and was not available from the Canadian textile mill. The result was that most of the fabric used in Canadian men's suit manufacturing was imported, and we had to pay duty on everything brought into the country. The duty on fabrics was a direct cost to the garment – it had to be paid even before the cloth arrived in the cutting room – and increased our selling price ten to fifteen per cent. How were we going to compete with suits imported from countries that had duty-free access worldwide to raw materials? Between duties, unions, and health and safety laws in Quebec, one manufacturer once told me that since he was importing the fabric he might as well make his life easier by importing the finished garment and close his factory in Canada.

As I understood it, duties and tariffs were supposed to protect domestic manufacturing. Why did we have to pay duty on raw materials not made in Canada? Who was the government protecting? This obsession with fabrics led me to an eventual battle with the Canadian Textile Institute (CTI).

During the seventies, while we were continually trying to improve our customer base and show our lines differently, the political situation in Quebec was changing. The Parti Québécois came to power and everyone around me thought the province would separate. (I was never worried, but many people were.) At that time, a garment factory in Winnipeg became available, so we bought it. The factory was able to make garments that would appeal to a new set of retailers. Besides, we needed extra production, and Quebec politics were crazy: buying a factory in another province was one way to avoid putting all our eggs in one basket. The province never separated and I eventually sold the factory in Winnipeg and lost one million dollars. Sometimes when you make a mistake, take your loss and move forward.

Through the seventies and eighties, my role on the Joint Committee led me to become more involved in representing the interests of the entire men's suit industry in Quebec. In the late seventies, since nobody else seemed interested, I was asked to become president of the Men's Clothing Manufacturer's Association of Quebec (MCMA) and vice-president of the Apparel Manufacturers Institute of Quebec (AMIQ). I took those roles not because I wanted power, but because I wanted to play a part in shaping the federal government's regulations impacting our industry. I long believed that what was good for the industry was good for Peerless, and that everyone would benefit.

To this day, I always make a point to advise business people to be aware of what's going on in their industry and especially how government policy-making affects their profitability. One should never assume that civil servants and politicians, those who make the rules and regulations, understand what is good for any particular industry. They can't possibly know every detail of every industry, and that is why a good businessman shouldn't be afraid to make his views known to every level of government whether federal, provincial, or municipal. In Canada, politicians are always available when you call them, because they want your vote and the votes of your employees.

By the time I took on the textile lobby in Canada I was armed with a lot of information and an intimate knowledge of how our industry was impacted by decisions made in Ottawa. What I didn't know was what was to come next.

9

David and Goliath:
My Battle with the Woven Textile* Industry

I was convinced that the men's suit industry was being crippled by the combination of finished garment imports and the tariffs and duties on all raw materials not made in Canada. I went up against the very powerful Canadian Textiles Institute (CTI) to have those tariffs and duties eliminated. I believed it was a necessary step for the apparel industry to survive and continue manufacturing in Canada.

On the one hand, the federal government was telling the apparel industry to compete with imported garments, but on the other, it was propping up the CTI with protectionist tariffs. We *couldn't* compete: our hands were tied. I did not want to start importing finished suits – I wanted to keep my factory running and provide jobs in Montreal. I sincerely believed that if I had duty-free access to raw materials not made in Canada, I could compete with imports.

At one point, I visited an Italian men's clothing factory that sourced from more than one hundred textile mills in Italy alone. The absurdity that one solitary Canadian worsted mill could possibly satisfy the needs of all domestic suit manufacturers became obvious. And because there was only one source for any specific textile product in Canada, that textile mill could set their prices

---

* My dealings were almost exclusively with the producers of woven textiles, not knitted fabrics.

up to include their tariff protection. There was no competition in the Canadian textile industry, and it baffled me that we had to pay tariffs on fabrics made elsewhere, ostensibly to protect a Canadian textile industry that wasn't competitive. The three giants – Dominion Textile (cotton and polyester fabrics), Dupont (nylon yarns), and Celanese (acetate yarns and fabrics) – lobbied the Canadian government to apply duties on imported fabrics. They depended on their close ties with the government to protect their generally inferior products. The CTI had a full-time office in Ottawa with lawyers constantly influencing our federal government. Their contention was that the textiles produced in Canada were *substitutable* for anything the apparel industry could buy internationally. They were wrong. None of the big three produced wool or wool products, and yet the CTI presented itself as representing the entire apparel industry (not just the textile industry) and Ottawa listened. This had been going on for close to seventy-five years. I thought the system was unfair and irrational, since it hurt the same customers that the textile mills relied on for their long-term survival.

Duties on textiles and trimmings for a men's suit were like a road map: there were duties on the findings inside the suit, on the fabric, on the shoulder pads, on buttons, on zippers, on linings, on everything. If the imported worsted fabric fell into a certain category of weight, it carried an eight-per-cent duty. On some synthetics and wool blends that duty could be twenty or twenty-two per cent. It drove me crazy. It made no sense for the federal government to effectively tell me who to buy from, especially when they were telling me to buy materials of a lesser quality than I could get elsewhere.

I had meeting after meeting with the federal government with a single goal in mind: stop the government-protected textile industry from killing the apparel industry. There were more Canadians employed in the apparel industry than in the textile industry; I was trying to protect apparel jobs. We needed to be unshackled from the prohibitive system of duties. I wasn't afraid to tell this to the government, and it made me an enemy of the domestic textile industry.

At that time, as well as there being only the one Canadian mill that made worsted fabric for men's wear, there was also only one Canadian supplier of trimmings and interlinings. We couldn't buy the fusibles and interlinings that we needed domestically – the quality wasn't good enough – so we imported trimmings from a German company whose representative, Raffi Ajemian, ended up working for us many years later. Raffi recalls what the landscape was like in those days:

Canada Hair Cloth, in Ontario, was the only Canadian manufacturer of haircloth canvas and fusibles, and they made old, obsolete, archaic stuff, the same way they'd made it in the 1950s. It was a solid fabric with no stretch. Their product would stay passive and not move. The German product had evolved over the years and as the fabrics became much finer, the Germans came up with a fusible product that stretched with the fabric.

I introduced it to Peerless, which was the first Canadian manufacturer to say, "Wow, we need this product." Maybe, if all the others had done the same, they would still exist today. Peerless brought it in from Germany and paid eighteen-per-cent duty on it. The tariff was there to protect just one business, Canada Hair Cloth, who did not even make a stretch product.

Of course, Canada Hair Cloth argued that given enough opportunity, they would eventually make the product. But to do so, they would have had to invest millions of dollars, which they didn't have. The German product was available at that moment and was more adaptable to the new age of fabrics, but Canada Hair Cloth kept saying, "We have something similar." Yes, it was for the same application, but it was not similar at all.

We went to Ottawa and appeared before the Canadian International Trade Tribunal (CITT) to testify that Canada Hair Cloth's product didn't do the same thing. "It doesn't stretch, so we can't buy it from Canada Hair Cloth." It was a long and expensive process, but we eventually won.

One of the reasons it was so hard to change the system was that for years, people, including bureaucrats in Ottawa, had lumped the textile and apparel industries together. In the early days, when I started my government relations meetings, I would introduce myself by saying I was in the men's suit business and bureaucrats would respond, "Oh, you're in textiles." I had to explain that not only were the primary textile and the secondary apparel industries two distinct entities, they often had very divergent interests.

Lumping the two industries together had worked for the textile industry since the early 1900s, and was something they continued to promote. The CTI had members that included yarn makers, knitters, textile finishers and dyers, and anyone who was connected to the textile industry – including Dupont, which was a chemical company producing nylon yarns. For a period of time, the head of Dupont became the president of the CTI. Before 1975, since there was no other association representing apparel manufacturers, the CTI spoke for us. It was our only option at the time, but it did not work well for apparel manufacturers. When the textile industry bragged about how many people they employed, they inflated their numbers by adding those in the production of knitted fabrics as well as those who worked in the apparel industry. Some knitters thought they were in the apparel industry and joined AMIQ (our apparel organization), and some thought they were in the textile industry and joined CTI under textiles. The CTI used this confusion to their advantage. (My issue was with the woven textile industry.) When the government finally woke up and heard the complaints of apparel manufacturers, it encouraged us to form the Canadian Apparel Federation (CAF). Textiles and apparel had to be separated once and for all.

As finished suit imports began to pour into Canada, the situation became critical. Now we were competing with suits made in places where wages were low and manufacturers didn't have to pay tariffs on anything. Canadian retailers began to place large orders from South Korea, China, Taiwan, Japan, and other low-wage jurisdictions. In order to prove our point to the federal government, we asked for emergency protection against dumping into the Canadian market. Given the tariffs we had to pay on raw materials not made in Canada, we couldn't compete. We never received protection, but I think it strengthened our position on the removal of tariffs.

It wasn't just about men's suits. The textile industry wanted tariffs on other fabrics coming into Canada as well. Every shirt fabric was either yarn-dyed or piece-dyed – either the yarn is dyed before it's woven or the fabric is dyed after it's woven – but there were no yarn-dyed fabrics made in Canada. Dominion Textile, which controlled the textile lobby in Ottawa, kept insisting that their piece-dyed product was *substitutable* for yarn-dyed fabric made elsewhere.

Because I was recognised as being involved with imported fabrics, I was put in charge of a subcommittee on textiles for the shirt industry. When we tried to get yarn-dyed fabrics declared duty free, an argument ensued between Dominion Textiles and the apparel industry. We brought in retail buyers to testify about their needs in front of the CITT in Ottawa. During the hearings, we proved that retailers and consumers could tell the difference between the two fabrics. After a lot of time and money spent on lawyers representing our case in Ottawa, the CITT ruled that yarn-dyed fabric was *non*substitutable. As a result, the yarn-dyed shirt fabric became duty free.

One victory at a time eventually wins the war.

We also had to fight Celanese about viscose lining. Viscose lining had to be used in the engineered suit, and Celanese only made acetate lining, which shrinks when pressed. I went to the president of Celanese and asked him to either make viscose lining or let it into Canada duty free. He replied, "You can use viscose when I tell you you can use viscose." It was like dealing with the Mob. They just weren't used to an apparel manufacturer encroaching on their turf.

Once again we went to the CITT, this time in an attempt to have viscose fabric ruled duty free. We quickly realized how difficult and expensive it was to deal with the CITT, which had been influenced by the textile industry into thinking Canadian textile manufacturers could produce everything the apparel industry needed. I believed that the federal government should find ways to simplify the process and develop new rules and regulations for complaints to be filed with the CITT. It took too much time and effort and was very costly to approach the CITT at that time.

I didn't know it then, but I would later have a great opportunity to alter this unfair system when the government needed my support, as well as that of the entire apparel industry, when trying to pass the Free Trade Agreement (FTA) in parliament. Sure enough, in 1988, in exchange for our support, the government introduced simplified rules and regulations with which to approach the CITT. This would eventually lead to changes that brought the Canadian apparel industry a step closer to competing with imports.

In the meantime, we had to find a temporary solution to our problem with viscose lining. Since viscose *yarn* was duty free (but *woven* viscose fabric was not), I made a deal with Doric Textiles to weave duty-free viscose yarn into lining at their mill in Quebec. It saved us the duty and made us more competitive, but the quality wasn't as good as what was available from European suppliers.

It took several years of pleading our case, but eventually we won. The CITT recommended that viscose lining be duty free if it was to be used for "end use men's fine clothing." The "end use" method was the only way we could convince the CITT to adopt our request, but it was confined exclusively to men's fine clothing. It was a method I'd learned of years before from my best friend, Lorne Abramowitz. He was in the neckwear business and was able to import silk fabrics duty free for the end use manufacturing of neckwear. The ladies' garment sector was irate with me because the new rule applied only to viscose used in men's fine clothing. They thought I was just interested in my own sector, but I believed one battle won was better than none and that the new rule would eventually be applied to their sector as well (which is precisely what happened some years later).

Canada was subject to bilateral agreements with various countries including Japan, South Korea, and China. The Canadian Textile Lobby's influence on these agreements led to low quotas on imported wool fabric. Because the quota was quickly filled, the exporting country could ship very little into Canada duty free, and fabric prices would rise because of the added duty.

By the mid-seventies, our federal government was being lobbied by every sector in the apparel industry – twenty-three different subsectors – and it was getting unwieldy. The government told the apparel industry to get together and speak with one voice, which led to the formation of our provincial group: The Apparel Manufacturers Institute of Quebec (AMIQ, now called Apparel Quebec). Other provinces also had their own organizations. KSA, recognized as the premier consulting firm in the Canadian apparel industry, recommended me to sit on the AMIQ board. This is how I became executive vice-president of the AMIQ, representing the men's suit sector. The federal government was so happy we'd formed an industry association that they paid for our first advisor, Peter Clark.

In 1984, the Trudeau government formed the Lumley Task Force on Textiles, Clothing and Trade. It was headed by the minister of industry and trade, Ed Lumley, and co-chaired by Ray Chevrier of Celanese (textiles), Peter Nygard of Tan Jay Clothing (apparel), and Sam Fox, Canadian co-director of the Amalgamated Clothing and Textile Workers Union (labour). I was the representative of the men's suit manufacturers in Canada.

At our first meeting, Lumley opened with, "OK, you guys have to work out your problems." The mandate of the task force was to provide the Canadian government with recommendations for a long-term development strategy for its textile and clothing industries. The task force had three major objectives. First, they called for maintaining a modern, efficient, and technologically competitive textile and clothing industry in Canada, and secondly, to optimize investment, production, and employment in these industries. Finally, the third objective was to increase the competition in Canada and abroad of quality Canadian-produced textile and apparel products.

It just happened that we started our meetings the same day Pierre Trudeau resigned as Canada's prime minister, 29 February 1984. Over the next two days I kept mentioning, at every opportunity, that we could sort out our problems if we didn't have to pay duty on fabrics not made in Canada. The representative of Dominion Textile said, "Mr Segal, we make 257 different fabrics."

In reality, they only made poly-cotton fabrics for the shirt sector, so I said, "I will make a suit for you, free of charge, out of any one of your fabrics, if you will wear it." He got very angry and sat down.

As the talks continued, I was invited to a dinner meeting with the co-chairs of the task force, including Celanese and the head of the CTI, at one of Montreal's old establishment clubs that didn't admit Jewish members. The meeting was meant to calm me down. They tried everything to convince me to stop saying the words "fabric availability" but, while I was still stuttering in those days, I stood my ground. Since I knew it would aggravate them, I waited till the end of the dinner to quote the AMIQ advisor Peter Clark: "The textile industry is an albatross around the neck of the apparel industry." They slammed the table – glasses clattering everywhere – before angrily storming out and leaving me alone with the waiter. I said to the waiter, "I hope they paid the bill because I'm not a member – I'm Jewish!"

In the development of the task-force work program, we established eight subcommittees. These were put in place to ensure that industry, trade, fiscal, and human resource policies were addressed, and that manufacturers of textiles and clothing, as well as labour and retailers, had the opportunity to contribute to all aspects of the strategy. I was appointed chairman of the apparel subcommittee on technology. At the government's expense, I was able to hire KSA, which wrote a report on how the apparel industry's long-term survival depended on the removal of tariffs on textiles not made in Canada. The day I submitted the report and passed it out at the task-force meeting, everyone started reading it immediately. Ray Chevrier glanced at it, and when he saw what KSA recommended he stood up and, in a loud voice, demanded that all copies be returned and destroyed. His words alerted some people in the room, and I watched as some of them hid copies of the report in their briefcases. The Canadian Textiles Institute did not want to consider that the survival of the apparel industry depended on the removal of fabric tariffs protecting their primary industry. The meeting immediately broke up.

On 16 July 1984, Ray Chevrier sent a letter to Peter Nygard saying, "The textile industry's position is clear on this issue and we will not entertain further debate on fabric availability; therefore, we are assuming that we will not have a consensus report for the final recommendation." Peter Nygard replied to the letter, pointing out that "Fabric availability remains a key issue that is dividing our two sectors and cannot be passed over without thorough investigation."

The textile representatives said they would never sit in the same room with me again. In effect, they had declared war on the apparel industry, their own customers. A year later, on 30 July 1985, a letter from John Mackillop, a government representative, was sent to all members of the task force. Essentially, the government was thanking us for our involvement in the task force. Mackillop wrote, "We have re-examined our mandate in the context of the current environment. In light of all circumstances, we have concluded that rather than continue the work of the Task Force, it would be in the best interest of the textile and clothing industries in Canada to concentrate our efforts on a long-term development strategy."

One evening, around the same time, a demonstration took place in front of my home in Westmount, Quebec. People were walking up and down the street and shouting insults, trying to make sure everyone in the area heard them. My wife got scared when some of the protesters pulled out flares, torches, and signs. They were ultimately trying to scare me off, demanding that I stop my demands on textiles. The commotion was so disturbing that I called the police and told my wife to blame the textile industry if I was ever in a "mysterious accident."

10

Trying to Survive

From the mid-seventies to the mid-eighties, while spending time in Ottawa fighting the textile industry on tariffs, I was also balancing the day-to-day management of Peerless with the requirements of our long-term viability. In addition, I was involved in changes to the Quebec Joint Committee and was actively representing the interests of the men's suit industry as president of the MCMA.

We were still in the process of transitioning our factory on St Laurent Boulevard to the engineered suit. I spent a lot of time integrating the new machinery we needed, while making sure the job descriptions for each operator fit within the rules and regulations of the Joint Committee. My right-hand man Ben Lipes and I were focusing on putting out two lines a year: spring/summer and fall/winter. We were also trying to install a new computer system in order to collect the proper information to build the company. Our ultimate goal was to create a better sales force and compete with imports, which was almost impossible. In fact, our major customers were starting to source their needs directly from East Asia. Times were tough, but it was a tremendous learning period for me.

In the late seventies, in order to properly exploit our advantages, we needed to upgrade our equipment. In 1979, we bought our first design and pattern-making computer system. Before the system arrived, we hired a student and trained him to operate the machine, but the week before it was installed he told me he'd been accepted to medical school and would be leaving. Coincidentally, my daughter Barbara graduated from Brandeis University in Boston at the same time. Although she already had another job offer, she did me a favour and came to Peerless to help with the installation of the new computer system. Barbara did so well on the installation and got so involved with the management at Peerless that what was meant to be a temporary job became a permanent one. She went on to become our systems analyst and was a tremendous help in designing the computer system for company operations. Barbara worked closely with me and became my sounding board on the future of the company. Barbara stayed with us for twenty years before moving on to focus on her growing family and return to school. She made a huge contribution to the long-term success of the company.

During this period when my life at Peerless was all encompassing, it was also a crucial time for me personally. After twenty-five years of marriage, Sandra and I seemed to have grown apart rather than together. We divorced amicably in 1982. Our children were all living out of the house, either at school or working, and both Sandra and I wanted to move on with our lives. We mutually agreed to separate without the need of lawyers, but hired one to represent us both when pleading our case in front of the judge. During the hearing, we were both so happy to be starting new chapters in our lives that our lawyer had to sit between us and "separate" us. He thought the judge wouldn't grant us a divorce if we looked too happy together. Sandra moved out of the house, and we agreed to sell it and divide all our assets. I will always be grateful to Sandra for raising our three wonderful children, taking care of our home, and helping me through all our mutual endeavours.

In the eighties, I tried everything to keep our factory on a full production schedule. To do this, we started a separate trouser company called "Pantco." When the factory produces suits things are fine, but when sport coats and blazers come into fashion, you have to start selling odd trousers to keep your pants factory working. Most suit manufacturers try to be in the odd pants business, but it is very difficult to compete with companies specializing solely in trousers. Pantco required us to hire specialists in the odd pants business with a separate sales force. We also had to set up two separate fabric inventories. Pantco lasted for about ten years, but was never profitable as a separate company.

Ben and I spent a lot of time calling in consultants to implement planning and better scheduling, constantly trying to make the factory more efficient. We did everything we could to keep the factory working, increase production, and make a profit. We even tried producing ladies' skirts and ladies' pants for a second time; we tried anything that could be made in our factory.

My background was the factory, and in some ways I never left it. That separated me from my competitors because I knew that if I solved problems based on what was best for the factory, I couldn't go wrong. It made us a manufacturing-oriented company and ultimately, a success.

Some lessons were more expensive than others. Once, while my controller/credit manager was on vacation, I was asked to approve an order ready to be shipped. This account, a Toronto retailer, had been on our alert screen for two seasons. We had been selling to him with the understanding that a payment was required before any shipment of merchandise. He agreed with this method and continued to order from us. From one order to the next, the client would increase the number of garments, so as to gain our trust. This time he asked us to make an exception, telling me on the phone that he would make full payment within the next ten days. He explained that he really needed the suits for a big sale he was having. I knew the account was risky, but after making several phone calls for references and looking at his purchase history, I approved the order. The day after receiving our shipment, the retailer declared bankruptcy and, because he was based in the province of Ontario, we had no recourse. I had just lost $175,000. A few weeks later a creditors' meeting was held and because I was the biggest creditor, I was named chairman of the creditors' committee. Sitting with me on the committee were only factoring companies who had insured the accounts of others. They knew I was extremely vulnerable at that moment because I was the only uninsured manufacturer at the table. This experience taught me that I'm a suit manufacturer, not a finance company. I had already paid for the fabric and labour; I wanted to get paid by my customers. I don't want to lose sleep at night.

Through that experience, I learned that most apparel manufacturers use a factoring company to insure their receivables. After a certain amount of time, if the customer doesn't pay you, the factoring company will. From that point on I started using factoring companies, but eventually we outgrew them. After some years, we began dealing with Export Development Canada (EDC), a crown corporation that encourages exports and, because we are a manufacturing company, guarantees all our receivables today.

One of our largest Canadian chain-store customers was taking more than nine months to pay its invoices. Since I knew the owner very well (his brother had been an usher at my wedding), I went to their head office in Toronto with the salesman in charge of the account. I told the owner we couldn't wait nine months or longer for him to settle his accounts. Back then, we required all payments within ten to thirty days and would set the price of the order accordingly. The faster a customer paid, the bigger the discount would be. I told him that at the price he was paying, we required payment within ten days. He started telling me how proud I should be to be dealing with him, because he was expanding his operation using our product in all his new stores. Finally, as I listened to his rationale, I lost my cool and said, "I want to get paid on time, and if you can't do that, you can take your order and shove it up your ass." My salesman nearly dropped dead; the commission on that account was almost half his entire income. We stopped dealing with the account for two or three seasons. A year and a half later, the customer came back and dealt with us properly, paying within thirty days. It's a weakness in selling; some apparel companies are so desperate to get their merchandise into stores that they give customers extended credit and special return policies. I wasn't going to build my business that way.

At the same time, we needed a long-term plan. In Canada, there weren't enough retailers to offer us room for growth. Three department stores – Hudson's Bay, Sears, and Eaton's – the retailer Dylex Limited, and the chain store Grafton Fraser were the big five buyers that were needed as customers to survive. We sold to all of them but still weren't growing. Canada just didn't have the customer base to generate the volume that would make for ultimate efficiency at our price point. We were sitting next to the biggest market in the world and we couldn't crack it, but I knew that was where we needed to be.

One time I went to the central buying office for many retailers in New York with a sample of my engineered suit. They took a look at my garment, crumpled it up into a ball, and threw it on the floor. "We can't sell that shit in this country!" I picked my sample up from the corner and went back home. I don't think I made a good impression. Better luck next time.

Our motto was "Canada's Best Value in Clothing," and value meant volume. The more limited a line is, the more efficient you are. You can't let your customers be your designers by offering them hundreds of fabric choices and dozens of suit styles. We tried to introduce a system we learned from Brookfield Clothing in the US called "item merchandising." It meant predetermining what the retailer would want. We narrowed our line and offered our customers much less choice, slowly revolutionizing our system. We were preparing for the future. It worked for two reasons: the value and reliability of the engineered suit and the Free Trade Agreement, which enabled us to produce on a massive scale.

As the quality of our garments started improving with the engineered suit, we ended up hiring a merchandiser from a company who sold at a much higher price point, and he introduced us to the finer fabrics needed to change the retailers' perception of us and get better gross margins. The engineered suit was so beautifully made that with finer fabrics, we could sell at a higher price point and be an even more profitable company. But our salesmen hit a wall because our customers couldn't envision Peerless producing a more expensive line. A customer once told me, "I buy suits made with the same fabric from a better maker. Your engineered suit looks just as good even though it's lower in price, but I don't want to kill my higher-priced line. You can't sell to both Eaton's basement and Harry Rosen if the suit is made on the same production line." To get around that mindset, I decided to start a new line that would cater to retailers needing higher-priced suits. I wanted to show our customers that Peerless could make a better product. Eventually that line grew, and we started a new production line in the factory. Since the engineered suit was well made and reasonably priced, we ended up in a niche somewhere in the middle. To this day, we still have two production lines in our Montreal factory, each making slightly different quality suits sold at different price points.

I continually tried to cut costs wherever I could to keep prices low. Before I took over as president in 1970, my old partners had increased our salesmen's commission from five to seven per cent in an attempt to boost sales. I had been against it, since it raised our prices, didn't increase our sales, and negatively impacted our competitiveness. Our competitors always paid five-per-cent commission to their salesmen, and I wanted to change our commission back to match theirs. When we cut our commission back, we also introduced a compensation package that was acceptable to the salesmen. What they were losing in commission, they would get as bonuses. As we gradually changed over the sales force, the bonus was phased out.

During the early eighties, my daughter Renee joined Peerless in the engineering and scheduling department after graduating from Clark University. Renee adapted very easily and became close to our factory workers. She made everyone feel comfortable by recognizing their needs and helping them. She was doing a great job, but after a few years decided to go back to university to further her education and become a science teacher.

In the meantime, Ben felt that he was under an enormous amount of pressure. He tried to pace himself and limit his work at Peerless, but he needed to take care of his health and couldn't do that as long as he still had responsibilities at the company. He decided to leave. He was always, and still is, one of my closest friends and, as it turned out, was better as an advisor than a partner. I often talked with him about Peerless, keeping him informed of the company's progress.

After Ben's departure from the company, I owned one hundred per cent of Peerless Clothing. This was never my long-term plan, but things just happened that way. I was very reluctant to take on

10.1 Ben Lipes and me, mid-1990s.

another partner because all my partners developed some sort of heart condition – which I hoped wasn't a reflection on me as the source of their stress.

I was still trying to break into the US market. Rubin Brothers Clothiers Ltd, a men's suit manufacturer located in Victoriaville, Quebec, had built half their sales in the US market. They had sold made-to-measure, custom-designed suits, but had just closed their doors. I knew their former president, Nick Philip, and thought he would be an asset in helping us make inroads south of the border. He joined Peerless to help me with my long-range plan. But Nick didn't fare too well. For every new account he acquired, he seemed to lose two. He would meet with US retailers, and as soon as they found out he was working for Peerless they'd say, "We can't touch your suits. Peerless doesn't have a recognized international union." Similarly, a potential customer once told me, "I love your product, but I can't buy it. My employees in the alterations department are part of the Amalgamated union, and they won't make alterations on Peerless Clothing suits." That's how powerful the sectoral union was in those days.

I knew it was a problem, but also knew we had a great product. A quartz watch sells for less than a handmade watch yet keeps better time. The engineered suit was like a quartz watch. It looked just as good as a tailored suit but without all the handwork. This made it a threat to traditional suit makers who were all part of the international sectoral union.

Breaking into the US market continued to be my goal. I knew we could do it; I just hadn't found the right contacts yet. In the mid-eighties I had a new opportunity, although I didn't recognize it at the time. Because of my position on the Apparel Manufacturers Institute of Quebec, I was invited to join a government-sponsored trade mission to Italy set up to help us learn how to be more competitive. The group included a jeans maker, a shirt maker, a dress manufacturer, and me. During the ten-day trip, we visited many Italian factories making different products. One day we were taken on a tour of a suit manufacturing company called Gruppo Finanziario Tessile (GFT) in Torino, Italy. I'd never heard of them before, and I told my companions, "Don't tell them I'm a suit manufacturer." I was afraid GFT wouldn't let me into their factory. They were making men's suits for Armani, Valentino, and Ungaro – all the best high-priced labels sold at retail in the USA.

As we walked through the factory, I saw that they were working the traditional Italian way, with a lot of handwork and tailoring. At the end of the line, I saw the final examiner of the Armani suit line reach back without looking, grab a jacket, try it on in front of the mirror, and pass it on before repeating his inspection with the next jacket. When he wasn't looking, I stealthily took off my Peerless engineered suit jacket and hung it on the next hanger behind him. Without realizing, he took my jacket and put it on while looking in the mirror. He looked carefully at the shoulders, the collar, the lapels, and approved my jacket. It was a great moment, and confirmed for me that I was on the right track with the engineered suit.

After the tour, we were invited by the export manager to have a coffee in their showroom and he told us the history of GFT. They had a large percentage of the high price point of the US market and were trying to get into the lower end with a label called "Profilo." I don't know what possessed me but as we were leaving, I gave him my business card and said, "I can show you how to get into the lower end of the US market." I didn't even know if the export manager had heard my statement, but to my surprise, two weeks later, two employees from GFT called me from Mirabel airport. They were on their way back to Italy from Asia and said, "You told us you'd show us how to get into the low-end US market at a $400 retail price-point." Luckily, my girlfriend at the time spoke Italian, so they stayed overnight in Montreal and we talked over dinner.

The next day I had the chance, while they were touring the Peerless factory, to show them how the engineered suit fit around the collar and shoulder. I knew they spent a lot of effort and time on this in their own factory, and we were getting the same results they were without all the hand tailoring. From the expression on their faces, I knew I had shown them something they hadn't seen before. For some reason Italy never adopted the engineered suit. That's why garments made in Italy are usually more expensive; they generally include more handwork.

A couple of weeks after their visit, I got a call from Guido Petruzzi, president of GFT in the United States. He said, "Please come to New York and bring a sample of your suits. I'd like to meet you." When we met, he handed me back the card I'd given the export manager in Italy and said, "You said you'd show us how to get into the American market at a popular price point." I showed him a sample suit and told him we could produce the suits in our Montreal factory, sew in the Profilo label, and charge him $125. He asked me to make a few changes to our product, which I explained we couldn't do. I told him our suit was made the same way their competitor, Hugo Boss, made their engineered suit, which retailed at well over $400. I walked out of his office with a promise that he would try it and ended up securing the biggest order Peerless had ever received. Peerless sold the suit to GFT for $125, they sold to the retailer at $200, and the suit retailed for $400. We scheduled production over the next two seasons. Because GFT sold their higher-priced labels to department stores in the US, they had an entrée to the same stores for their popularly priced line. At the time, my management team in Montreal was very sceptical because we hadn't been able crack the US market, but I knew we would rise to the occasion.

Meanwhile, the twenty-five-year lease I had signed in 1962 was due to expire in 1987. Everyone knew free trade was coming, and with it I believed my dream would finally come true: we would break into the US market. But in order to go forward, Peerless needed more space. Since I already rented more than half of the building at 9600 St Laurent Boulevard, I went to the owners with an offer to purchase the entire building, but we couldn't make a deal. In hindsight, thank God they turned me down! It ended up being the best thing that could have happened, because the building would have been too small anyway.

I was tired of dealing with landlords, and I wanted to own and build my own factory building. (In my next life, I'm going to be in the real estate business and be a real success!) I took out a three-million-dollar mortgage for ten years and another three million for twenty years. It was a big decision, and some people thought I was crazy, but to me it was not a risk at all. American manufacturers were paying forty-per-cent duty on the same wool fabric I was using in the Profilo suits. Even with the twenty-two-percent export duty I was paying to the US government on my finished garment, because I got the duty back I paid to the Canadian Government on all my raw materials, I knew I would be able to compete with or without free trade.

We found out there was city-owned land available in the northeast part of Montreal on Pie-IX Boulevard. It was a working-class neighborhood, and I knew there would be a steady supply of factory workers in the area. The city of Montreal had a development incentive program and was offering the land at a very low price on the condition that we build a structure. I made a deal with a company called Divco to be the general contractor, and we designed a building similar to the one I had seen in Italy when I visited GFT.

When we started the plans, I bought a ten-dollar compass and stood on the corner of 39th Street and Pie-IX Boulevard with my contractor, the late Sam Aberman, owner of Divco. Knowing what direction the sun would rise and set, as well as the direction of the wind, helped me design the layout of the building. I decided to put the shipping doors and cafeteria on the east side of the building. Since the shipping and receiving doors are kept open for most the day, I knew we couldn't put them on the west side because with the wind coming from that direction it would be too cold in the winter. I also wanted the cafeteria on the east side so that our employees could enjoy the sun in the morning and at lunchtime. With this building, built almost thirty years ago, we have been able to accomplish enormous growth and success.

In designing my dream building I had the help of our plant manager, a young civil engineer in his mid-twenties named Oreste Pendenza. We bought an architectural software package that Oreste was familiar with, and we designed the new factory's lay-out together. During the planning phase I would dream about the layout at night, come in the next morning, tell Oreste about my dream, and we would review the layout together before putting it on the computer. He was very good at logistics and planning.

At the ceremony for the ground-breaking of the new plant, my old friend Stan Kivenko from Jack Spratt Jeans pulled me aside and said, "Why the hell are you mortgaging yourself to the eye-balls? Free trade is going to kill you. Take the money and go buy yourself a Ferrari. Don't you see the world is changing and you can't compete?" I said, "No, Stan. There's going to be an eruption of opportunity under the Free Trade Agreement." I saw opportunities where other people saw obstacles.

The difference between Stan and me was that he manufactured jeans made of cotton denim fabric. Since the fabric he was using was produced domestically and available in North America, he would be vulnerable under free trade. My advantage was that the wool-worsted fabric we used was not available in North America and I

10.2 The ground-breaking ceremony for our new factory on Boulevard Pie-IX. In the foreground, Moe, me, and my daughter Barbara, with shovels, 1987.

knew that, for anything exported under the FTA, we would not have to add in the cost of duty on imported raw materials. As Stan recalls, "We were all saying to Alvin, 'You're going to move into a new factory with free trade coming?! You won't be doing any sewing once it's here.' Alvin had terrific insight."

The cost of our new factory came in below budget because we did all the planning and layout ourselves. After two years of hard work, continually working hand in hand with our contractor, Divco, we finally had four walls, a roof, and 300,000 square feet that we filled with the latest equipment for making the engineered suit. It included 100,000 extra square feet for future expansion. I wanted to have at least one tenant in the building because that would make it illegal for a union to picket outside our front door. I was lucky to rent 50,000 square feet to the federal government, which put in an unemployment insurance office. It sounds great, but a new problem developed as a result. During lunchtime, our employees would run down and look at the board to see if there were any better jobs available in the area. Fortunately, we didn't lose too many employees.

The whole thing was a huge investment, but it was a well-calculated risk made in anticipation of the changing economic landscape, one that I thought would drastically alter the playing field in our favour. I always kept in mind our future US sales opportunities and planned accordingly.

Just before we moved, during the last week of March 1988, I brought Moe Segal, who was then in a wheelchair, to see the new building. Since he was always against my investing in my own building, I told him that I was renting from the bank. I didn't want his last days to be spent worrying. Moe passed away a few weeks later, at the age of ninety. Once again I had lost a father, who I considered to be a confidant and a great supporter.

In April 1988, over the Easter long weekend (it was actually April Fool's Day, but I'm not superstitious), we moved into our new plant. It was a long and tiring four-day weekend, but we were up and running on Tuesday morning. We did not lose one unit of production. I supervised the move, and my team helped me set up the new factory. Everything worked according to plan.

Next we needed a warehouse in the United States to service GFT properly and facilitate shipping. We had a choice between the states of New York and Vermont. Vermont, although a longer drive, was a better state to do business in, since it had a lower tax base and was also less prone to union pressure. I was introduced to the Franklin County Industrial Development Corporation. We found them extremely encouraging and helpful in locating a warehouse space, an accountant, and a lawyer. They found us a 7,000-square-foot warehouse to rent in Fairfax, Vermont, just twenty minutes south of the Quebec border.

Knowing that free trade was eventually coming, we formed an American company called Peerless Clothing International, wholly owned by the Canadian company, Peerless Clothing Inc. Now, Peerless Clothing International could sell directly to American retailers in US dollars and ship from our Vermont distributing center. We would eventually hire an American sales force, enabling us to give excellent customer service without having to deal with

10.3 With my children, Joel, Barbara, and Renee (left to right), circa 2003.

customs' issues at the border. Our American sales team wouldn't have to do the paperwork of international trade or deal with currency exchange issues.

Over the years, as our business expanded and we needed more space, we moved from Fairfax to St Albans, Vermont. Again with the help of the Franklin County Industrial Development Corporation, we settled in St Albans Industrial Park in a 14,000- square-foot space that had enormous potential for growth. Step by step we took more space in that building, and when we had occupied all of it we built a second one attached to it. Customer service has always been our primary focus, and this pushed us into adopting better computer and inventory systems to meet the demands of our customers. This has really separated us from our competitors. Our Vermont location has expanded over the years to include three more buildings (all interconnected) and now occupies well over a million square feet of space.

In 1989, after graduating with an MBA from Columbia University and having worked on Wall Street for three years, my son Joel joined the business. He married and moved to Montreal with his new bride, Eileen. They planned to have a family and wanted to raise their children in the Montreal Jewish community. I was very happy he was moving home. With his Wall Street experience, Joel was a perfect fit (pardon the pun) for our management team in Montreal. He quickly understood that we needed to do business in the US to ensure our long-term success.

11

The FTA Is Coming

After a lot of rumours, in mid-1985, negotiations finally started for what would become the Canada-US Free Trade Agreement (FTA). Many Canadian industries were worried that big American companies would put small Canadian ones out of business. The Canadian government wanted advice and input from all those industries in Canada that would be impacted by the FTA and formed Sectoral Advisory Groups on International Trade (SAGITs) for each industry. Because of the textile-apparel war – which I had been deliberately fuelling at every opportunity, including while on the Lumley Task Force – the government had the wisdom to finally separate textiles from apparel. On our own SAGIT, we could talk to government about the flawed system of duties on textiles, which had to be changed once and for all.

On the apparel SAGIT, I represented men's fine clothing. Joe Schaffer and Elliot Lifson represented ladies' dresses, Peter Nygard represented ladies' sportswear, Oscar Rajsky represented the shirt industry, Jack Kivenko represented the cotton jeans industry, and Claude Lapierre represented the lingerie industry. There were others on the SAGIT representing additional sectors of the apparel industry as well.

Regular SAGIT meetings were held for three years, and I gathered a tremendous amount of knowledge throughout the proceedings. At the very outset, I was introduced to the words "imports" and "quotas" and began to gain a full understanding of their meaning and importance to our industry. Fabric availability was in the interest of every sector represented on our SAGIT. We could finally get down to ensuring access to fabric and raw materials without contending with the textile industry's agenda.

During the SAGIT negotiations, it became very clear that the apparel industry needed access to raw materials not made in North America to compete with free trade. US retailers didn't need more of what they already had; they needed something new. All sectors of apparel manufacture – from ladies' lingerie to dresses and ladies' outerwear to men's clothing and outerwear – had the same problem: access to sufficient varieties of fabric to meet the demands of North American fashion retailers. Because our company had transitioned into producing wool suits, my issue with tariffs was all about wool. Wool was the fabric of choice in the men's fine-tailored clothing sector, and the biggest input cost in a men's suit.

As the sole representative of the men's suit industry on the apparel SAGIT, I made duty-free access to wool-worsted fabric a key demand. I made it clear to our federal negotiators that we wanted duty-free access to the hundreds of mills in Italy and the rest of the world. This would enable us to compete in the US. The textile and wool lobbies in the US had tremendous influence over the US free trade negotiators. In one meeting, one of the US negotiators stood up and, gesturing with his hands, said, "Canada is going to become a funnel for wool suits coming into the US market." Wool textiles was their major focus, and it became a potential deal-breaker for the US negotiators, who insisted on imposing a quota on all types of garments coming into the US from Canada, even though their main concern was men's wool suits.

My battle cry, dating back to the Lumley Task Force almost ten years earlier, was "Duty-free access to raw materials not made in Canada," and it brought negotiators to an impasse. I became the key spokesman for the apparel industry on fabric availability, an issue particularly crucial to the men's suit business. US negotiators really only cared about protecting the American textile industry, primarily the wool textile sector. Their team didn't seem to care about apparel makers in the US that weren't using wool. At the eleventh hour, US negotiators imposed a quota on garments coming into the US that used imported textiles not made in North

America. Wool was such a sensitive issue that the Americans ended up with two separate quota categories: one for wool and one for every other fabric used in the other sectors of apparel.

A similar quota was imposed on apparel coming into Canada from the US. The Americans had the same opportunity with their quotas, although it was never utilized. Under the quota system, every garment made of fabric foreign to North America was measured in square metre equivalents (SMEs) per garment, not by quantity of garments. Quota depended on how much fabric was used. A suit had five SMEs, a jacket had three, and a pair of pants had two SMEs, and so on. The entire wool quota in the FTA represented less than two per cent of the US retail suit market. Peerless's production at that time could have used the entire Canadian wool quota. I tried to demand more quota, but the US negotiators wouldn't agree. To me this meant that the FTA wasn't free trade at all, but a protectionist trade agreement favouring the textile industry.

The apparel SAGIT committee also decided how the export quota would be divided among Canadian manufacturers. The only experience we had was with the apparel quota system used in Southeast Asia, so we copied it: if a company exported a certain amount of SMEs in one year, the government gave them the same SME quota for the following year.

We had another major advantage under free trade. Since many other industries in Canada were against the FTA, the Canadian government needed the support of the apparel industry, which was a major employer. By this time, I was a very important voice on the apparel SAGIT, and I saw this as an opportunity to have some long-hoped-for changes made. I was able to convince my colleagues to support the government passage of the FTA on condition that the CITT's unfair system of rules and regulations was clarified and simplified in order to remove the duties on fabrics not made in Canada. To secure our support for the passage of the FTA, the Canadian government offered apparel manufacturers the extraordinary provision of duty-free access to fabrics for five years, as a period to adjust to free trade. However the government had one important condition: manufacturers would receive duty-free access only on raw materials scheduled for export to the US. Offering US retailers fabrics they didn't already have was crucial for the success of Canadian apparel manufacturers in the new market. To this day, I am very proud of my part in making this happen; it changed the way apparel manufacturers operate in North America.

As talks continued, the FTA was scheduled to come into force on 1 January 1989. No one in the industry knew which companies would win or lose when it came into effect, but I was intent on being one of the winners. Looking back, it would be easy to attribute Peerless's success to simple good fortune. Yes, a lot had to do with timing. However, making the right choices during the late seventies and early to mid-eighties placed us in a position to take advantage of the dramatic changes that came with the FTA. I wasn't just flying on hunches; a lot of strategic planning had gone into the choices I made.

One important factor was that we didn't have to negotiate with an international union to make changes to our factory. Since we had our own legally approved union, the Fraternité des Travailleurs de Vêtements pour Hommes or the "Fraternité," we had been able to produce the engineered suit much sooner and more easily than our competitors. The Fraternité was certified by the Quebec Department of Labour but still unrecognized by the Amalgamated international union (then called UNITE), which was desperate to take over the Fraternité.

As well, I had learned a lot about import and export tariffs, duties, and quotas from my colleagues on the SAGIT. The slow transition we made over the years from manmade fabrics to wool, in order to improve the quality of our suits and get them into a better segment of the market, turned out to be one of the smartest business decisions I ever made. Historically, because wool worsted fabric was sourced from the British Empire, Canada had a favourable duty rate on any wool products coming from the UK (under the British Preferential Tariff, BPT). Canadian manufacturers paid eight-per-cent duty on British wool while Americans paid forty-per-cent duty on the same fabric. This meant that Peerless had a distinct advantage even before the Free Trade Agreement. Under the FTA, so long as there was available quota, we would pay no duty at all on our suits entering the US. That gave us an incredible advantage over US suit manufacturers. Additionally, our labour costs were down because the Canadian dollar had weakened against the US dollar, and, as a result our product was even more competitive.

We had a fabric advantage, the right product, and no international union stopping us from making changes. It was the perfect combination of ideal conditions and unique opportunities. I went away for my Christmas holiday knowing that 1 January 1989 would be the start of a new era for Peerless. But in my wildest dreams, I never imagined how high we would fly.

12

The Missing Link in the Chain

On 1 January 1989, the Free Trade Agreement was in force, our new factory was up and running in Montreal, and the men's suit industry was operating in a financial sweet spot with no import tariffs on raw materials for five years for garments exported to the United States. It seemed like the stars had aligned beautifully for our position in the industry, and I was in a state of euphoria. All my dreams and everything I had worked so long and hard for was falling into place. I could hardly believe it. It was like being in love.

The quota system worked beautifully for Peerless because we were already exporting Profilo suits to our warehouse in Vermont. But the quota was small and each manufacturer's future portion would be based on their previous year's shipments. That fact, coupled with the new duty-free status on imported wool fabric, made me determined to ship our entire Canadian production to the US. All my focus went to producing and shipping suits to the US; I stopped caring about my Canadian customers. Even though we had no orders for additional suits above the GFT order, we put the factory into high production, shipping as many suits as we possibly could to the US, and filling our US warehouse in order to establish more quota. I knew we would find a customer to buy the suits at a low price. Building quota was more important in the long run than the profit we would make on those additional suits.

All Canadian suit manufacturers knew what the rules were, but in hindsight I realize they didn't fully recognize the opportunity available to them. As president of the MCMA, I called a meeting

12.1 I was seated on a panel next to Louis Laberge, head of the FTQ, at a Montreal conference at the start of the FTA, 1989.

at the former Montreal Montefiore Club and tried to explain to my members the opportunity we all had. The subject of how the FTA would affect the men's apparel industry in Quebec also came up at a Joint Committee meeting. The suggestion was made that the JC hire a consultant to conduct a study. I said there was no time to do a proper study and predicted that the quota would be filled within a year. The wool quota was only two per cent of the entire American retail suit market. "Peerless could absorb the entire Canadian quota all by itself. I'm already shipping my suits. By the time you guys do a study, I'll have taken the entire quota."

I did what I could to fulfill my responsibilities on both the MCMA and the JC, but nobody took me seriously. A consultant was hired, but by the time his final report came back (a year or so later) there was no quota left, just as I'd predicted. By the end of the first year of the FTA, on 1 January 1990, Peerless had more than eighty per cent of the entire Canadian wool-fabric quota for the US market, and my Canadian competitors were furious.

Nobody had expected one company to corner that much of the Canadian quota.

However, just because free trade was in place, I couldn't show up in Times Square with samples and start hawking garments; American retail buyers weren't waiting for a new source of suits from Canada. Like most of my Canadian competitors, I had underestimated the scope of what it would be like doing business in the US under free trade. We had no contacts among US retailers and no insight as to what changes had to be made in our styling and scheduling for the US market. We needed a US sales team that could rise to the challenges presented by all these opportunities. The launch of free trade was like the firing of a starter's pistol with Canadian manufacturers not knowing which way to run. It was like starting a brand new business

On a trip to Palm Springs in February of 1989, I happened to meet up with my old friend Herman Soifer, who had taught me so much about the men's suit business when he ran Brookfield Clothing in New York in the early seventies. I hadn't seen him in many years, and I was so proud of our new factory and of how far we'd come with the engineered suit that I invited him to Montreal. A month later, he accepted my offer and came for a visit. I showed him around the factory and took him to the cutting room where we had recently installed computerized machines replacing most of our cutters. I explained how free trade had changed everything and what an advantage we now had, especially over US manufacturers. After ten minutes of walking through the factory, he grabbed my arm and dragged me into my office where he said, "Alvin, you have a tiger by the tail, you just have to tame it. No one can touch you, but you've got to hire a great salesman in the US." I figured Herman knew everyone in the US market, so I put him on a retainer with a mandate to find someone to handle our US sales.

Around that time a new opportunity – which could have been a disaster – arose when our factoring company pulled the line of credit insuring our major Canadian customer, Grafton Fraser. Grafton Fraser accounted for almost half our Canadian sales. Losing them knocked me on the head. (Grafton Fraser was subsequently restructured and is one of our active accounts today.)

The factor's decision forced me to get on the plane to New York the next day. I was going to deal once and for all with my one American salesman. He had to bring in a lot more sales or I'd be looking for someone else.

On the plane, I met one of our import textile suppliers from Montreal, Jean-Paul Longlade, who gave me a lift into the city and invited me to see his new office in the same building we occupied at 1290 6th Avenue, where many men's clothing companies were based. At his office I met one of his representatives, Moe Moses, with whom I'd dealt years earlier when I was buying fabric. I told him that I was looking for a salesman for the American market. He grabbed his phone and said, "I've got the perfect guy for you."

A few minutes later, in walked Ronny Wurtzburger. As I shook his hand I started to say, "My name's Alvin Segal and I'm from Montreal." Before I could finish Ronny said, "I know all about you. You're making the Profilo suits for GFT." He knew that because he represented an Eastern European importer who also sold tailored suits in the US market. I told him I was looking for someone to run my US sales and without skipping a beat, while we were still shaking hands, he said, "I could make you the biggest manufacturer in North America, but I'm not an administrator. I'm a salesman."

I was impressed by his passion and ambition. I said, "Fine. I'll administer. You sell." Before we'd even broken the handshake, it seemed like we had an agreement, but the contract had yet to be negotiated. I had no idea that moment was the most crucial turning point in the history of Peerless Clothing. Herman Soifer happened to be in New York that day, so I called him to tell him I had just met someone who could be perfect for the job.

"Ronny Wurtzburger?!" Herman said, in apparent disbelief that I'd found the guy he'd been looking for. "I've known Ronny since he was a kid. He's a great salesman. He can sell anything."

"Herman," I replied, "That's exactly what we need."

I took them to lunch and it turned out they had known each other for more than thirty years. In fact, their families had been fighting each other in court for many years. Ronny's grandfather had owned a company called Eagle Clothing, and after it went under Herman started using the name for a new clothing label at Brookfield. Lawsuits ensued and the whole thing dragged on for years with no settlement. Over lunch that day, they decided to end their litigation.

I'd finally found a guy I liked. Ronny had all the right qualities we needed. He knew everybody in the industry on the US side, and I liked the way he saw the big picture. But he wanted a contract. Back in Montreal when I told my lawyer and accountant this, they both said, "Don't sign a contract, you don't know the guy." However I'd had a good feeling about Ronny from the moment we met, so I signed a contract, confident that if it didn't work out, we'd find a way to end it.

I agreed to pay him what was quite a lot of money at the time. I remember playing golf with my friend Jeremy Reitman at Elm Ridge and telling him how much I was paying Ronny. Jeremy, who ran the Reitman's clothing chain, said, "Alvin, don't worry about it. If you pay peanuts, you get monkeys."

When it came to selling, Ronny Wurtzburger was no amateur. He turned out to be by far the best salesman and merchandiser I've ever known. Straight out of college in New York City, Ronny had joined Eagle Clothing, the family business, where he learned from the bottom up. He started out in the fabric sponging department (shrinking the fabric), did stints in the cutting room and the shipping department, and then found his niche in merchandising and sales. He was with Eagle for twenty-odd years, working his way up the ladder by being aggressive.

It was a tough environment. Even though his family owned a third of the business, the uncle who ran the company after Ronny's grandfather passed away wasn't easy to get along with. Ronny had to earn everything he got. He eventually became head merchant, then took over running a division and made it into the biggest part of the company before Eagle went into Chapter 11 bankruptcy protection. The banks asked Ronny to take over and throw his uncle out. He didn't want to do that, but before he left, he arranged a takeover by another company. According to Ronny, "I secured my parents and my uncles, and I left with zero in my pocket. I'd had a lot of promises before, but I left with zip." Ronny added:

I decided that imports were starting to sell, and I wanted to get to know that market so I joined an import company in the early 1970s. They made inexpensive suits, sports coats, overcoats, pants, and raincoats. They were in the same opening price point of the market as Peerless. I became president, and within two years we had a forty-five-million-dollar clothing business in the US, bringing in imports from Eastern Europe. I found myself spending a lot of time in Romania, Czechoslovakia, and Hungary – really learning. It was a different kind of merchandising: you had to lay out your own fabrics and work within those confines. They didn't have all the colour yarns that you wanted, so you had to work with what they had. It was a great experience, and I stayed with them until I ran into Alvin Segal.

He's a very determined man; he can play coy all day long but when he wants something he ends up getting it. He kept calling and trying to put a deal together. I kept saying "I don't know," he kept raising his offer, and finally it got to the point where I couldn't say no to him.

I signed a contract with Ronny that had a base salary and an override on increases in sales. He came to Montreal to meet my general manager, Nick Philip, who was also our fabric buyer. It was August 1989, and Nick showed him the range of fabrics for our fall 1990 line. The first thing Ronny said was, "Where is your plain gabardine range? It's the main fabric I'm using this season with my customers." Nick said, "Gabardine is very difficult to tailor, and we don't show it in our line. We can't tailor it properly." Gabardine was used by the makers of higher priced suits but not those at Peerless's price point. However, Ronny sounded so convincing that I told Nick, "Bring in a length of gabardine, and with our engineered tailoring system, it should be easy to tailor, and it should look great." I knew the engineered coat system would solve the problems experienced in traditional tailoring.

A few weeks later, Ronny saw the sample and couldn't believe how beautiful it looked. Ronny knew what we didn't know: that this fabric was exactly what we needed for the US market. The gab suit became the Peerless Clothing "signature" suit in the US.

When I gave Ronny the first price list, he said, "Your prices are too low. Are you sure you're making a profit?" Ronny had been buying the same fabrics, but hadn't known that we had a cost advantage because of the FTA quota and because we paid no duty. He looked at our product and said, "Raise your prices. I'm a salesman. I can get a better price for what we're selling." I had never heard a salesman tell me that I should raise my prices, which made me realize that Ronny was also a businessman.

The first account Ronny approached was one of our existing customers, the retailer April Marcus. Ronny booked a new order, selling our suits at higher prices than Nick Philip. After Ronny left, a representative from April Marcus called Nick in Montreal and complained, which resulted in Nick giving them a discount. Ronny found out and called me right away. "Either Nick is in charge of US sales or I am." I told Nick that Ronny would have complete control for all the US sales and would report directly to me from that moment on.

Ronny told me how he wanted to build our sales team. These were all new ideas to me, but I had Herman Soifer as my consultant to backstop Ronny's ideas. Ronny knew everyone in the business, and was able to assemble a sales team in no time. Just before the 1989 Christmas vacation, we agreed on two new salesmen who would get a draw towards their commission. We then closed for the two-week Christmas holiday. At the first sales meeting in early January 1990, Ronny showed up with eight salesmen – it seemed he knew every suit salesman in the United States. I said, "There were only supposed to be two guys!" But I trusted his judgment and hired them all. Some of the salesmen he brought with him are still with Peerless twenty-seven years later.

Ronny eventually built a US sales force of twenty people, each responsible for a different part of the country. When they started, they all wanted an advance on their commission because they were giving up the lines they had. I didn't think twice about it because Ronny was so confident that we were going to succeed. Ronny recalls:

> Not to brag, but I happened to have a great reputation, and I started going after all the best salesmen in the industry. I must have interviewed 150 guys to cover the whole country. The guys I hired would go to the retailers in their marketplace – at that time we were not selling to any department stores – and they would say, "Listen, Ronny Wurtzburger is joining Peerless Clothing and he tells us it's a great product. Would you give me an order?" The retailer was sold before he even saw the sample, because the guys we put together were seasoned pros who were the best in their territory. They were doing OK in their old jobs, but they saw this as a great chance. They figured that if I left where I was to go to Peerless, there had to be something at the end of the tunnel. And so we came up to Canada with all these fabulous guys.

Nick stayed on as our fabric buyer, which resulted in a fiasco when he substituted a lower priced piece-dyed gabardine fabric for the yarn-dyed fabric our samples had been made with. Two months later when Ronny and the salesmen saw the suits coming out of production, they realized the fabric had been switched, and the suits looked totally different from the original samples. It was a disaster, and we had to get rid of the suits. Nick should have known better and when he realized he'd made a terrible mistake, he walked out of the company without saying goodbye. However, he did leave me a message that read, "You are on the right track. You don't need me anymore." By leaving, Nick made it easier for me. I had brought him into Peerless to develop our US sales, and now we had Ronny making my dreams a reality.

Nick's departure left an opening for my son Joel to take more responsibilities in the business operations, the costing, and the fabric buying. Joel understood from the beginning how to analyze and work with the data we had, doing a great job with the business operations and the costing while Ronny concentrated on the selling. With Joel and Ronny working as a team, Peerless became even more profitable. My son's involvement in the company gave me confidence that our future would be remarkable.

Ronny would walk into a store and ask the retailer to try our product. We were essentially selling Italian piece-goods at unheard-of prices, and in less than three weeks we sold out our entire production. In those days, we were selling a Peerless suit bearing the store label. As Ronny recalls:

The prices were unbelievable. I was scratching my head as to how we could do it, but it was free trade that was making it so inexpensive. As good as I am in the selling part, Mr Segal was that good on the inside. It was a magical mix because he was an expert – he believed in making a garment a certain way that nobody else really believed in at that time and the garments were coming out like soldiers, every single one looked exactly the same. *Beautiful.* When we first started shipping, everybody loved what they were getting because every suit looked the same. It was like the army when you see them marching. We were getting rave reviews from our customers.

We had a very small office in New York when I first started. Then, the office space beside the elevator became available, and it was right next door to us. We rented the space and extended our offices. Being right next to the elevator was a big deal, everybody would see us. So I called Mr Segal and said, "Listen, I am going to have a sign guy come and make a sign for us." He said, "Don't do anything, I'll be there in a few days." Well, next week the chairman of Peerless comes down with his plastic sign and a little toolkit. He made the sign and he hung it himself. To this day, I never told him that it was a little more to the right than it should have been. We also needed racks and he said, "I'll be back next week." He got racks for the showroom and hung them for us himself. That's the kind of person he is.

The combination of free trade and Ronny Wurtzburger joining Peerless at that crucial moment made the company what it is today. The opportunity was huge because the US market was ten times larger than the Canadian one. We had all our pieces in place, and there was nowhere to go but up. The growth we experienced over the next few years was explosive. In his first season (six months), Ronny replaced Grafton Fraser's sales, which was more than half our production. We were hiring like crazy to keep up with demand. Ronny and his team would tell retailers that we could only sell them 150 units as a test before the season launched, and they'd turn around and ask for 300.

We were still making suits for GFT, so I told Ronny, "Don't tell your customers that your orders are being made in the same factory." Ronny replied. "Oh, Mr Segal, I would never tell my customers that." I didn't believe him for one minute, but I thought that if GFT can sell suits to American retailers, so can we.

Now we needed support in the Montreal customer service department for Ronny and his sales team, so Joel hired a woman named Claire Saad in August 1990. She recalls our highly memorable first meeting:

I answered the ad and came in to meet with Joel. After interviewing me, he said, "I want you to meet my dad," so I said, "What do you do here?" He replied, "I'm the owner's son." I saw at that point that it wasn't a very structured environment. Mr Segal walked into the room and said hello and introduced himself. He then asked me, "What the fuck do you know about clothing?" So I answered, "Nothing, but I'll learn." It was pretty funny. It didn't affect me at all. I told him, "If you're trying to scare me off, it's not working." They hired me as a customer-service clerk. I was entering orders and doing clerical work, and I went to Joel and said, "This isn't what I was hired for." They didn't want to ruffle any feathers, so they said, "Don't let anybody know, but in time you'll be a customer service manager." This is how they do business … At the time, they'd just started doing business in the US, so it was booming. The company was growing faster than the manpower they had. They'd get 800 orders from the US and were writing them down on scrap paper. In order to have proper follow-up, I created a form and some structure. Then, we started hiring people because the number of calls was too crazy. This was 1990 and we couldn't keep up with the demand. It was this Canadian manufacturer who was taking over the market in the US wool suit business. We started having these huge sales meetings. At that time, it was all specialty stores; we didn't have any department stores as clients yet. We were flying.

Claire's right – it was crazy in those days. That was when we were madly shipping unsold suits to our Vermont facility just to build quota. It was like the Wild West. When Claire arrived, we had one customer-service clerk. Claire probably hired twenty people in customer service – anybody with good people-skills and a pulse. She started hiring people over the phone. We were building a whole new Peerless, aimed almost entirely at the US market, which Ronny was taking by storm.

One of the first changes Ronny made to our sales-meeting schedule was to advance the seasonal meetings three months earlier than they were. Ronny realized that we were shipping late, and by advancing the sales meetings we could buy the fabric earlier and improve the delivery of our orders. This fit perfectly with our 30 September fiscal year-end. Additionally, we hired a new fabric-buyer named Darrell Henson. Darrell had experience with better quality fabrics, which was exactly what we needed in order to cater to the needs of the US market.

Dealing with GFT had given me the confidence to sell Peerless suits in the US market at a higher retail price point. Now they were upset because Ronny was selling our product in the same fabrics to customers already carrying the Profilo label. His strategy was to emphasize that our suits were made in the same factory as the GFT product. GFT didn't renew their order, but by that time, Ronny had enough new orders to replace both GFT and Grafton Fraser.

By our fiscal year end, 30 September 1990, I was in such a favourable position with orders going forward and was so sure that the next year was going to be profitable that I learned another valuable lesson the hard way. Without telling the bank, I took a huge reserve on my year-end 1989/90 inventory in order to clean up old fabric that I still had in stock. That resulted in a substantial loss in the books for the year-end 30 September 1990.

During this period the apparel industry was very weak, and banks were getting out of the industry. When the Republic National Bank saw that my company was showing a loss without them having been warned, they sent me a letter saying, "We're cancelling your line of credit and are giving you thirty days to find a new bank." When I got the letter I couldn't believe how ridiculous it was and didn't take it seriously. I was so confident in the future that I left it the hands of my controller, who said he'd handle it. I went on a trip to Israel figuring the problem would be solved when I returned to Montreal.

A month later, I got a duplicate letter from the Republic National Bank, so I figured I should resolve the issue myself. They stated that they were giving us another thirty days before pulling the line of credit unless we made an immediate cash deposit of two million dollars to cover the previous year's loss. I looked at our forward orders and was baffled by the bank's decision. How could a bank make such a stupid assessment? I went to Toronto Dominion, with whom we'd dealt ten years earlier before we got a better deal with Republic National. TD looked at our financial statement, came to the same conclusion, and turned us down as well. They didn't care about how many orders we had going forward. They just cared about what our last year looked like.

I learned an important lesson. Don't surprise your bank. If you're going to show a loss (even one you plan for a good reason) tell them beforehand, so that you're both on the same page.

There we were, in the best position the company had ever been in, and turned down by two banks. I was shocked by their decisions but I was still very positive about the future. I knew the situation didn't make sense, and I knew that we would find a solution. Out of the blue, I got a phone call from a mystery lender offering to loan me enough money, at the "friendly rate" of eighteen per cent, to cover the two-million-dollar shortfall at the bank until our new orders were shipped. I didn't hesitate, because I knew that it would be only for a very short period. I just wanted to move forward and didn't care where the money came from. I never found out who my pricey benefactor was, but now, thinking back, it probably was the bank itself. They knew they would lose more money by closing us than by keeping us in business. To this day I don't know for sure.

Ronny recalls,

> When I tell you he's different from everybody else, I mean it. In order to stay alive, he was borrowing money at some unbelievable rates. He was basing his repayment plan on when we were shipping goods. He knew what we were going to make on those garments and how fast we were going to turn and get collections. He wasn't afraid. I always kid him that he has ice in his veins. He was as cool as a cucumber. I was nervous, and it wasn't even my money. I could go get another job …

Meanwhile, I had a deal with Ronny for his first bonus. He knew that I was struggling and that I was under pressure from the bank. Ronny remembers:

> We were getting many compliments from our customers and everything was wonderful until the end of the first year. My deal with Mr Segal was that I would get an override on the sales. A few months went by and I said to my wife, "What should I do; he hasn't offered to pay me my money?" She said, "Well, ask him." So I called him on the phone, and I asked him, and he was very honest. He said, "We don't have the money." So I said, "Let's sit down and see what the problem is and we'll fix it."

Ronny told me, "Keep my bonus – you'll pay me next year." That's how confident we both were that we had a bright future ahead of us.

At the same time one of my closest personal friends, Ernie Hirscheimer, was winding down his company and offered to invest his money in Peerless at a more favourable interest rate. That allowed me to get out from under the other loan at eighteen per cent. Ernie had been helping me, as my advisor and confidant, since I had bought my partners out years earlier. Republic National Bank was placated. However, they were also now constantly looking over my shoulder to make sure I was making a profit going forward.

Ronny was generating more orders than we could meet at our existing capacity, so we built an extension on the new factory to increase production. Both our auditors and the bank were furious; they told me not to spend any more money. They wanted me to slow down and didn't want me to invest in a company that had showed a loss the previous year. The bank sent their New York VP, some guy with an MBA, to lecture me and give me advice on how to run the company. As I was listening to him, I was playing with a paper clip. He must have made me lose my cool because, before I even realized it, I untangled the paper clip and threw it at him saying, "I don't know what you're talking about! Who are you to tell me how to run my company? If you don't like it, we'll change our bank."

Shortly thereafter, I received a call from our auditor. He had prepared our last year's statement and wanted to review it with me. He started telling me the same thing the bank had told me: "Stop spending money. Slow down." I ended the meeting by saying, "Enough! You're talking about the past; can't you look at the future? I want a new audit partner." It seemed as though everyone around me wanted me to stop spending, but I knew what the next year was going to look like and I knew the extension would be required to fulfill all the forward orders we had.

After moving in to the first extension, we had to build a second extension on our factory almost immediately to continue increasing production. Peerless was essentially being transformed into an American company with its headquarters and factory in Canada and its sales office and warehouse in the United States. The only space left was the one we had leased to the federal government for an unemployment insurance office. I went to Ottawa to meet with the minister of labour to let him know that I needed the space they were occupying. Their lease wasn't over yet, but I was willing to pay them to move to another location. The minister said, "Mr Segal, people get on their knees to rent space to the

12.2 The first extension to our Pie-IX factory under construction, 1992.

federal government and you're willing to pay us to move out? That's never happened to us before." They moved out soon after, and we took over the space.

Ronny and his sales team were selling so phenomenally in the US market and I was so obsessed with getting quota that I forgot about our Canadian customers. I basically started treating our sales operation as one market. If we could sell in Canada what we were producing for the US market, fine. Otherwise, it wasn't worth the trouble. Our Canadian salesmen weren't happy, but today we have one sales meeting for both markets and we sell the same product on both sides of the border. The merger of the sales teams was a logical evolution that made good business sense. Today, many Canadian retailers travel to our New York office to place their orders with our American sales team.

One day, I received a call from an American consultant who had been hired by the American Clothing Manufacturers Association (ACMA). His mandate was to find a way to get duty removed on textiles for US suit manufacturers the way we had in Canada, and he wanted my opinion. He asked me, "Alvin, how did you get the duty removed on fabrics not available in your country?" I told him, "First of all you have to separate the apparel industry from the textile industry. Because we were able to do that in Canada, we had easier access to the Canadian International Trade Tribunal, which listened to our requests and helped us deal with our need for fabrics not made in Canada." I said, "I doubt you'll be able to get the duties removed on fabrics the same way we did, because the US doesn't have anything like the CITT dealing with the government on international trade practices."

I was told a major suit manufacturer in the US was trying to compete with us in their market and, after analyzing our Peerless suits stitch by stitch, had concluded we weren't costing properly and would soon go out of business. They didn't realize that we were using duty-free raw material and our costs were much lower than theirs.

From 1991 to 1994, our US sales grew so much that Peerless Clothing surpassed Italy as the largest source of suits imported into the US. This was exactly what the US negotiator at the SAGIT had predicted ten years earlier: Canada became the funnel for men's suits entering the US. Had the US lowered their duties on textiles as Canada did, this might not have happened. As Ronny likes to say, "No one saw us coming. No one quite knew what hit them."

Knowing that our five-year duty exemption on raw materials would end in 1994, I continued fighting the textile lobby in Ottawa to have the duty permanently removed on fabrics not made in Canada. The report I had submitted to the Lumley task force in 1984 was coming true. In it, KSA had written that if Canadian suit manufacturers had duty-free access to raw materials not made in Canada, they would be able to compete successfully in the US market. Back then it had seemed like a dream, but in 1994 it was becoming a reality.

By representing and defending our industry in Ottawa, I ended up building a great company and, at the same time, assured the future of the industry that I love.

As for my personal life, in 1990 a friend introduced me to Leanor Segal, who would later become my second wife. She had been married to Moey Segal, the late Phil Segal's youngest son. Although I knew Moey, I wasn't invited to their wedding because they got married during the period when I was *persona non grata* with the Segal family. Leanor and I decided to get married in 1992 and began building our new life together. I started taking more time off from work to be with my new bride. As I slowly phased out from the everyday workload at Peerless, my son, Joel, took on more responsibilities.

13

Hard to Stay under the Radar

Thanks to free trade, we were selling so many suits in the US and were becoming so successful that we'd gone from "Nobody saw us coming," as Ronny had said, to "Everyone's aiming at us." We had become the largest men's wool suit manufacturer in North America. Somebody at the Wool Bureau Inc. (a branch of the International Wool Secretariat) told me that Peerless bought more wool suit fabric worldwide than any other privately held company in the world. Since the mid-eighties, our staff and factory employees in Montreal had quadrupled to over 3,000 people, and we had enlarged our Montreal factory building twice to reach the size of ten football fields. Every day by 4:00 pm, 7,000 suits were shipped to our Vermont warehouse. The equity of the company was doubling in value every year.

Meanwhile, our list of enemies seemed to be growing by the day. The overall number of suits sold at retail in the US was not increasing; we were obviously taking market share away from unionized US manufacturers and importers. Amalgamated suit manufacturers on both sides of the border were angry with us for taking so much of the FTA quota. We had more than eighty per cent of the entire Canadian wool quota, which was worth $25 million a year based on the duty saved.

The International Union of Needle Trades, Industrial and Textile Employees (UNITE, formerly the Amalgamated union) was incensed that we were expanding across the US and taking business from their unionized shops. UNITE was unhappy that a

13.1 View from above of our warehouses in Vermont, 2013.

single Canadian company had gained so greatly from free trade, and argued that it was never intended that one company would benefit that way. Under the FTA's dispute settlement mechanism, using the argument that the quota was meant to be evenly divided amongst suit manufacturers, they tried to file an international complaint. They thought the US negotiators had specified in the FTA that no single manufacturer could capture a majority of the quota, but they were wrong. This was never specified in the FTA and Canada, being a sovereign country, had allocated the quota according to its own rules.

Wool suit imports from Canada to the US rose by nine times between 1989 and 1992. At Peerless alone, we were taking in more than one million dollars a day in gross sales. When the Canadian dollar dipped to near eighty cents US, in the early 1990s, our advantage grew even greater. (The Canadian dollar was worth $0.87 US in 1991 and kept dropping until it reached the low $.70s in the mid-1990s.) We couldn't compete with imported suits in Canada because we had to pay duty on imported fabrics staying within the country, but in the United States our low prices made Peerless suits seem like they were produced in a third-world country.

In the meantime, the sales offices of the men's suit industry in New York moved from 1290 6th Avenue to 1350 6th Avenue, three blocks up the street. The industry had always stuck together, setting up offices in the same building and all signing the same master lease, in order to offer a "one stop shop" for buyers. By that time, Peerless had created so much excitement that the sales teams of other suit manufacturers wanted to stick close to us. Maybe they hoped some of our good luck would rub off?

As our business was growing, we couldn't afford losses on new accounts we knew nothing about. To ensure prompt payment of our shipments in the US (to customers we didn't have a sales history with), we continued doing business with Export Development Canada (EDC). They encouraged Canadian manufacturing companies to export by insuring and guaranteeing their receivables at a very low rate. Our bank was very pleased because they knew we'd collect our money no matter what. This also allowed us to grow without losing any sleep at night.

When Canada, the United States, and Mexico began expanding their three-way talks to negotiate the North American Free Trade Agreement (NAFTA), the Americans saw it as an opportunity to correct what they thought were errors they'd allowed into the FTA. Following the explosion in wool suit imports, the Americans wanted to change the rules for the entire apparel industry, but Peerless was really their main target. UNITE's members were primarily wool suit manufacturers, and they were all struggling to compete with us.

The negotiations for NAFTA became very hot and heavy during 1992 and 1993. NAFTA became a political football in the United States with articles appearing in all newspapers. The *International Herald Tribune*, the major English daily in Paris at the time, released one of many articles about the deal on 11 August 1992. They ran a front-page story with the headline, "An American Pact

An American Pact That's Hard to Sew Up

Success of Canada Men's Suit Firm Has U.S. Balking on Free-Trade Accord

By Clyde H. Farnsworth
New York Times Service

TORONTO — Peerless Clothing Inc., a family-owned suit maker in Montreal, has done so well in shipping its men's wool suits to the United States that it has emerged as one of the final stumbling blocks in the lengthy negotiations for a free-trade agreement involving the United States, Mexico and Canada.

In the last three years, Peerless has tripled its sales, to 100 million Canadian dollars ($84.4 million), and it now provides 80 percent of all the Canadian men's wool suits shipped to the United States.

Because of its growth and that of some other companies, the American textile industry has persuaded American negotiators to try to keep curbs on imported apparel. The Canadians have resisted, and the haggling continued as negotiations in Washington resumed Monday.

Another roadblock to an agreement was a last-minute quarrel over whether Mexico would allow American and Canadian companies to compete for certain contracts from Pemex, Mexico's state-owned oil company.

[Unsettled issues included: determining to what extent a car must be domestically built before it can receive duty-free treatment; establishing a system to settle disputes among the three trade partners, and ironing out some copyright and patent issues, Reuters reported.]

Commenting on the U.S. stand on apparel imports, Jack Kivenko, president of the Canadian Apparel Manufacturers' Institute, said:

"As soon as we have any degree of success — even though the amount of our exports is minuscule in the U.S. market — the Americans are trying to stop us, which is not really fair."

The U.S. trade representative, Carla A. Hills, has so far been unwilling to make an exception for Canada.

U.S. imports of men's woolen suits from Canada rose ninefold, to 456,000 in the 12 months that ended May 31, from 49,000 in 1987. That growth was largely a result of the dismantling of barriers under a free-trade agreement between the United States and Canada that went into effect on Jan. 1, 1989.

Peerless, whose 300,000-square-foot computerized plant employs 1,300 people in the north end of Montreal, saw the trade liberalization coming and capitalized on it. The 73-year-old company turns out 17,000 men's suits a week.

See TRADE, Page 6

13.2 The *International Herald Tribune*, 11 August 1992. Headline of an article by Clyde H. Farnsworth.

That's Hard to Sew Up: Success of Canada Men's Suit Firm Has U.S. Balking on Free-Trade Accord." Peerless had grown so far, so fast, that we were getting global attention for being a bilateral irritant.

In August of the same year every newspaper had at least one article on NAFTA, and they mentioned Peerless. In fact, the *International Herald Tribune* was only one of many papers to print a story about NAFTA and the role Peerless Clothing played in the negotiations leading to the final agreement. "Ottawa Says It Will Walk Out If NAFTA Deal Not Palatable" was one of the headlines from the *Globe and Mail*, "Pandering to Protectionists Clogging Free-Trade Arteries" (August 1992, *Wall Street Journal*), "Trade Talks Bog Down over Dispute on Apparel" (4 August 1992, *New York Times*), "Canadian Firm Feels Threat from NAFTA Textile Lobby" (6 August 1992, *Journal of Commerce*), "Canadian Trade Success Is an Issue for the US" (10 August 1992, *New York Times*), "Talks Snagged on Wool Suits from Canada" (10 August 1992, *Ottawa Citizen*).

At the eleventh hour, "The Watergate 300," a group of negotiators from Mexico, the United States, and Canada, took over the Watergate Hotel in Washington to finalize NAFTA. One of the negotiators, Andrew Shoyer, remembers all the employees from the hotel pulling out the furniture from the rooms and setting up chairs in a circle for the meeting. According to Shoyer, recently

Canadian Trade Success Is an Issue for the U.S.

By CLYDE H. FARNSWORTH

Special to The New York Times

TORONTO, Aug. 9 — Peerless Clothing Inc., a family-owned suit maker in Montreal, has done so well in shipping its men's wool suits to the United States that it has emerged as one of the final stumbling blocks in the lengthy negotiations for a free-trade agreement between the United States, Mexico and Canada.

In the last three years, Peerless has tripled its sales, to $100 million (Canadian), and now provides 80 per-cent of all the Canadian men's wool suits shipped to the United States. Because of its growth and that of some other companies, the American textile industry has persuaded Amer-ican negotiators to try to keep curbs on imported apparel. The Canadians have resisted, and the haggling con-tinues as negotiations in Washington remained unresolved today.

Canada's International Trade Min-ister, Michael Wilson, standing up for Peerless and other companies in the small but vocal Canadian apparel in-dustry, argues that Washington is clamping down unjustly on success.

Minuscule Market Share

Jack Kivenko, president of the Ca-nadian Apparel Manufacturers' Insti-tute, complained, "As soon as we have any degree of success — even though the amount of our exports is minuscule in the U.S. market — the Americans are trying to stop us, which is not really fair."

The United States trade represent-ative, Carla A. Hills, has so far been unwilling to make an exception for Canada.

Imports by the United States of men's woolen suits from Canada rose ninefold, to 456,000 in the 12 months that ended May 31, from 49,000 in 1987. That growth was largely a re-

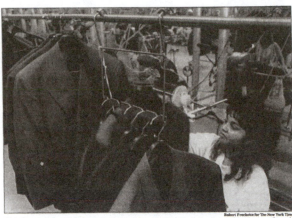

One of the stumbling blocks in talks for the North American Free Trade Agreement is the success of Peerless Clothing Inc., a family-owned garment maker in Montreal whose suits are popular with American retailers.

Robert Frechette for The New York Times

sult of the dismantlement of barriers under a free-trade agreement be-tween the United States and Canada that went into effect on Jan. 1, 1989.

Peerless, whose 300,000-square-foot computerized plant employs 1,300 people in the north end of Montreal, saw the trade liberalization coming and capitalized on it. The 73-year-old

company turns out 17,000 men's suits a week, as well as trousers and sport jackets.

Its chief executive and principal owner, Alvin Segal, a 58-year-old Montreal resident who calls himself a manufacturing specialist, said he had prepared for expansion by turning to a process known as European engi-

neering to make what look like hand-tailored suits without the hand tailor-ing. Instead, pieces of fabric are care-fully molded and fused to garments.

"When I saw what the Europeans were doing, I was fascinated, and

Continued on Page C3

13.3 The *New York Times*, 10 August 1992. Headline of an article by Clyde H. Farnsworth.

interviewed on radio, there were people everywhere, in each room and down every hallway. Writing about the Watergate 300 for a National Public Radio (NPR) program, Stacey Vanek Smith said, "In one room people were arguing about sugar, in another room, cars, in another room, textiles. Ron Sorini, only thirty years old at the time, was in one room. He was the chief textile negotiator for the US. The issue threatening the trade deal? "Wool suits from Canada." Ron Sorini remembered, "I was ner-vous because I knew that my issue could potentially be the one to derail the agreement."

Before the FTA, no one thought of Canada as a major exporter of men's suits. Peerless's success woke up the entire apparel indus-try and became a significant factor in the NAFTA agreement. The final negotiations at the Watergate Hotel were supposed to be com-pleted over two days, but continued for two weeks because of the wool suits issue. "Every day Sorini would sit in a little room

Since 1989, Peerless Clothing has flooded the U.S. market, where it has 1,300 retail accounts for its cheaper versions of top-line suits. Says owner and CEO Alvin Segal: 'We are a victim of our own success.'

(TOM HANSON/The Globe and Mail)

TRADE / *Entrepreneur Alvin Segal has cut such a wide swath in the U.S. men's wear market that the American textiles lobby wants to shut him down*

Canadian suit firm threatens to unravel NAFTA talks

BY BARRIE McKENNA
Quebec Bureau
Montreal

ALVIN Segal probably has more riding on the current North American free-trade talks than just about anyone, including George Bush and Brian Mulroney.

Mr. Segal's **Peerless Clothing Inc.** is little-known outside the rag trade, although his company is quite familiar to Canadian, U.S. and Mexican negotiators sweating over the final points of a North American free-trade agreement. Peerless has made such a stunning foray into the United States that a few thousand of Mr. Segal's suits are now threatening to hang up a continent-wide free-trade deal affecting billions of dollars of trade.

"It was not exactly expert planning on our part," said Mr. Segal, president and majority owner of the Montreal-based apparel manufacturer. "We are a victim of our own success."

As recently as yesterday, trade negotiators huddled in Washington for the final sprint to the North American trade deal were still haggling over suits. U.S. negotiators are reportedly pushing for strict limits on imports of Canadian-made suits in exchange for allowing greater access for other Canadian clothing.

PEERLESS CLOTHING

Head office: Montreal

Employees: 1,300

Founded: 1919

Annual sales: Over $100-million

Owner and CEO: Alvin Segal

Locations:
Plant in Montreal (300,000 sq. feet)
Warehouse in St. Albans, Vt.
Sales office in New York

Major products: Makes 17,000 men's suits a week plus pants and sport jackets

Exports: 90% of sales in the U.S.

Rank: Canada's largest maker of men's suits

Peerless, a private company with annual sales expected to exceed $100-million this year — more than three times its 1989 sales — has come out of nowhere to become a victor in the 1988 Canada-U.S. free-trade agreement. (The firm is not related to Montreal-based Peerless Carpet Corp.)

Exports of Canadian-made men's wool suits to the United States jumped to 380,000 last year from 50,000 in 1988. Peerless, alone, accounted for as much as 80 per cent of those suits, worth a total of about $50-million last year, Mr. Segal said.

The company's success seems so elemental, it is a wonder others have not followed suit, as it were.

Since 1989, it has flooded the U.S. market, where it now has 1,-300 retail accounts, with cheaper knock-offs of $1,000 German-made Hugo Boss or Italian tailored suits.

The Peerless version is sold to stores for as little as $130 (U.S.) and retails for up to $400.

The catch is that Peerless employs almost no tailors, having replaced them with an array of computer-assisted cutting, sewing and gluing machines.

Please see SUIT — B5

13.4 The *Globe and Mail*, 5 August 1992. Headline of an article by Barrie McKenna.

drinking coffee and going through the latest draft of the textile deals with the Canadians and the Mexicans," wrote Smith. A multibillion-dollar trading agreement was being held up by wool suits! The US negotiators wanted the number of suits coming into the US duty free to be very limited, if not eliminated completely. They felt that the competition between Canada and US suit manufacturers was getting too intense. Mike Wilson, Canada's minister of international trade, recalls a US colleague saying, "All I can find in my tailor shop in Washington are Canadian suits made in Montreal." The US negotiators wanted to level the field, because companies like Hart Schaffner Marx had to pay more than a thirty-per-cent tariff to import wool textiles from Italy, while Canada could import the same fabric duty free.

The fact that Peerless was located in the province of Quebec, where there was always the threat of separation, contributed to Ottawa's support for us. Peerless was a star player in the apparel industry. Ottawa was very proud of that and didn't want to undermine the success of a business that employed so many people in the province.

As NAFTA negotiations were getting close to completion, I received a call from Michael Wilson's office. It was a Friday afternoon and his secretary told me, "Stay by your phone over the weekend. Mr Wilson wants to get your personal opinion on the terms for your industry being negotiated in NAFTA." I stayed by the phone all weekend, but no call came. On Monday morning, while I was in the factory, my phone rang. I answered, but could barely hear anything despite my hearing aids.

"Hello Alvin, it's Mike Wilson."

"Mike who?" I could hardly hear with the background noise.

He repeated, "Mike Wilson, the international trade minister."

I ran to the door where I could hear better, and said, "Yes, Sir."

"Alvin, you're becoming more famous than I am," the minister said to me. "I want your opinion on our final terms of the NAFTA agreement. We were unable to get any additional quota."

I told him, "I'll be happy, but my competitors in Canada will not. The terms leave no room for them to sell competitively in the US market." The very powerful US textile lobby persuaded the

American negotiators to keep the existing quota and slap a twenty-four-per-cent duty on any excess above it. The Canadian negotiators, on the other hand, wanted to double the quota. Wilson had fought on our behalf, but the US side insisted on keeping the quota as it had been under the FTA, with no increase. Since Peerless already had more than eighty per cent of the existing quota there was little opportunity for other Canadian manufacturers to export duty free on finished garments, as there was no unused quota. When negotiations ended, the deal was set so that a maximum of 1.4 million wool suits per year could be imported to the US duty free. At a trade show in Toronto I once met one of my Canadian competitors. He said, "Alvin, we hired a consultant to do a study on why you've been so successful in the US, and we're ready to *plunge* into the market with you." I said, "My friend, there's no quota left. Good luck."

The textile industry had convinced NAFTA negotiators to make the rules of origin for the definition of a men's suit so complex that instead of being a free trade agreement, NAFTA provided protection for the textile industry. Not only did the fabric have to be cut and sewn in North America, but the fabric's yarn had to be made and woven in North America as well. In essence, they imposed a "triple" rule of origin. A true free trade agreement would have defined the rules of origin as follows: Buying the fabric from anywhere in the world and then cutting and sewing it into a suit in Canada results in a *substantial transformation* of the original product (the fabric transformed into a suit). However, that wasn't how the rules of origin were defined. Not only did we have to buy North American fabrics, we also had to buy the lining within North America. The only problem was that the lining we needed for our garments wasn't available in either Canada or the United States. Jack Kivenko (Stan's brother), who was president of the Canadian Apparel Manufacturers Institute at the time, told the *Globe and Mail*, "The Americans made it clear that Canada would have to sacrifice its apparel industry as part of the price for obtaining a NAFTA deal."

When NAFTA went into effect in January 1994, we worried that Mexico would become the new entry point for clothing into

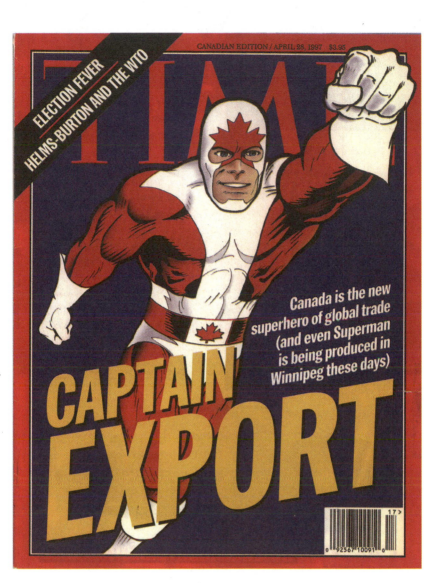

13.5 *Time* magazine cover, 28 April 1997.

the US market. I knew that when the agreement between the US, Mexico, and Canada came into force, there'd be a new quota out of Mexico. So before it took effect, I visited a men's suit factory that was for sale in Mexico City. Labour was cheaper in Mexico, so that was another good reason to inquire about a new plant there. During my visit, the owner's father, without realizing why I was there, asked, "Mr Segal, why can't we compete with Peerless in the US market?" It turned out, having learned from the FTA, US negotiators managed to keep the quota for Mexico very small. It didn't make sense for Peerless to expand into that country, and we didn't buy the factory in Mexico City. So much for the worry about Mexico!

NAFTA didn't really slow us down. When it came into force on 1 January 1994, we had already exceeded the quota and were paying the twenty-four-per-cent duty to the American government on about a third of our garments exported to the United States. From 1992 to 1997, apparel exports to the US – mostly in men's tailored wool clothing – more than doubled in value. We even made it into *Time* magazine with the following cover page, "Captain Export: Canada Is the New Superhero of Global Trade." In the *Time* article, "Trumps in Suits," the reporter told our story and described the struggles we endured during the years between the FTA and NAFTA. In fact, those years were extremely difficult for most American suit manufacturers, and many had to close their doors. Had they been able to overcome their textile lobby, as we did in Canada, maybe they'd still be in business today.

No one benefitted from the trade agreements more than Peerless, but after almost twenty-five years, certain parts of NAFTA have become obsolete and the agreement should be brought up to date. If ever the agreement is renegotiated, I hope to be at the table to ensure that the best interests of the men's suit industry in Canada are taken into consideration.

14

1991–2000:
Entering the Twenty-First Century
with the Rainmaker

Our struggles were far from over. The American-controlled union UNITE represented the suit industry in both the US and Canada, and since our share of the quota was so big, we were seen as a threat to its members. UNITE opened an office next door to our factory on Pie-IX Boulevard. They staffed that office with American organizers who tried to convince our employees that they were not being treated fairly by their own independent union, the Fraternité, though our employees thought otherwise. UNITE was ultimately trying to put Peerless out of business so that our quota could be passed on to other Canadian manufacturers, who were all members of UNITE. Most of our employees recognized what was going on; it scared them, and they did not want anything to do with UNITE.

After infiltrating our factory on Pie-IX, their campaign came to a head in December 1995, when forty of our employees filed thirty-six complaints with the Quebec Labour Board about working conditions at Peerless. Twenty-six of those charges were dropped. Two months later, the same group of employees filed thirty-four complaints of racial and sexual harassment with the Quebec Human Rights Commission – phony charges that were never even investigated.

The same forty employees who had signed with UNITE were then encouraged to hold demonstrations against us outside Eaton's and The Bay in downtown Montreal. Both department stores were major buyers of our private-label suits. To embarrass and harass us further, 300 protesters held a noon rally in New York outside Macy's flagship store at Herald Square in June 1996. Their protest received a lot of coverage on New York radio and television, which made it appear as if Peerless operated some kind of illegal sweatshop in Canada.

Nothing was further from the truth. In fact, the Montreal *Gazette* published a long feature article in which it noted that, despite the company's rapid expansion, there had never been a substantiated complaint from Peerless workers about working conditions in the plant. On the contrary: the province's Commission de la Santé et de la Securité du Travail (CSST) had cited Peerless for its excellent work-safety record, while the city of Montreal had praised us for hiring and promoting members of minority groups.

At one point, UNITE followed us to the semi-annual men's wear trade show in Las Vegas, to which we invite our customers twice a year. When we got off the plane, we saw billboards displaying negative advertising about Peerless. At dinner the first night we heard a whistle blow, and a man in a tuxedo, who had sneaked into the room, started yelling things about how bad we were. Our customers were very angry and it was they, not us, who threw him out.

The next day, because UNITE is an international union and part of the American Federation of Labor and Congress of Industrial Organizations (AFL-CIO), the local international union in Las Vegas organized a demonstration at our tradeshow. We heard a roar and approximately 300 noisy protesters marched towards our booth holding signs and yelling. The customers who were working with salesman in our booth weren't bothered a bit, and continued placing their orders with us. The police came, and the demonstrators were removed.

In another incident at that trade show, UNITE hung an enormous sign over the parking lot showing four of our Montreal employees with masking tape over their mouths and a caption underneath reading: "We were fired for speaking the truth." Their mistake was that they put the words "Peerless Clothing" in huge letters, while you could hardly read the caption. As a result, our customers thought it was a Peerless advertisement. One customer even doubled his order because he thought it was a great ad.

The campaign even spread to San Francisco, where the city council, controlled by the international union, threatened to pass a resolution denouncing us. They never succeeded, and we didn't lose a single order. In fact, the publicity probably helped promote our product.

Meanwhile, US clothing companies and labour groups were petitioning President Bill Clinton to renegotiate NAFTA in order to eliminate our advantage. During Clinton's second term re-election campaign, he was invited to make a speech at the biennial convention of the AFL-CIO. I got a call from a friend who was in the banquet hall for the occasion saying, "Alvin, you won't believe this! During Clinton's speech, UNITE passed around a hat to help the unions fight Peerless Clothing!" I'm sure the president wasn't aware of the fundraising drive, but US trade representative Charlene Barshefsky held talks with the Canadian Trade Minister Art Eggleton, who continued to defend us. Any action against us, he said, would be a breach of NAFTA and would trigger a dispute settlement case against the US.

In December 1995, UNITE tried to convince our workers that their union, the Fraternité, was controlled by management, but they failed. Under Quebec labour law, they had a thirty-day raiding period during which they could legally replace our independent union if they could get a majority of our employees (fifty per cent plus one) to sign membership cards. They didn't even bother to call for a vote. After spending millions of dollars, they complained that it was too hard to communicate with our factory workers because there were thirty-five different languages spoken among them. The reality was that UNITE was getting nowhere. When they tried to claim that the Fraternité would be better off under UNITE, our workers didn't believe them. They didn't want to lose their Christmas bonuses and the pay they received for Jewish holidays and other advantages UNITE didn't offer.

UNITE finally ended their campaign when the Fraternité signed a contract with another international union, the Teamsters. The Teamsters were affiliated with the Quebec Federation of Labour

(FTQ) and had a "no raiding" clause in an agreement with UNITE. The Fraternité contract became the Teamsters contract, and our employees kept the benefits they already had and didn't have to worry about any more interference from UNITE. It was a smart move by our workers. By that time, Peerless was the largest North American manufacturer of men's tailored suits, and because our employees joined the Teamsters union, UNITE's domination of the North American men's tailored clothing industry ended. It was probably one of the most significant turning points in the men's suit industry in North America. Could it be that all this happened because Peerless paid its employees for Jewish holidays?

At that time Peerless's factory workers represented more than sixty different cultural communities and was one of the biggest stumbling blocks UNITE encountered in its attempt to take over the union representing our workers. For many, Peerless was their first job upon entry to Canada; most would stay with us for many years. When we learned several of our employees would be taking the oath of citizenship, we thought it would be very meaningful to hold a citizenship swearing-in ceremony at our factory cafeteria. We approached Barbara Seal, a good friend and a citizenship court judge, and with her help (and the approval and participation of our union) a ceremony was held on 23 September 2004 during which more than twenty of our employees became new Canadian citizens. It was the first time that such a ceremony was held at a privately owned company in Quebec. It was attended by family members and friends of those being sworn in and was a great inspiration to all our employees who packed the factory cafeteria.

As sales in US specialty stores continued to grow, Ronny introduced our first label, "Kasper," which gave us entry to the major department store business. Soon after, Ronny connected with Ralph Lauren, which brought us our first international label, "Chaps by Ralph Lauren." We then realized the importance of international labels, which led us to where we are today. If I thought the FTA and NAFTA were turning points, signing licensing agreements with labels of international names created an explosion of new opportunities. Retailers, and certainly department stores, are

14.1 I stand next to Judge Barbara Seal during the citizenship ceremony held at Peerless in 2004.

willing to pay more if a garment has an internationally recognized label. By forming these new relationships with designer labels, Ronny became Peerless Clothing's "rainmaker."

As our explosive growth continued, so did our management challenges in Montreal. Most urgently, we needed to upgrade our computer system, which wasn't powerful enough to handle the boom in sales. We started with a new warehouse inventory system for our facility in Vermont. Because we had to go live too early and didn't do proper testing, the system didn't recognize where the garments were located in the warehouse and things went downhill fast. I wish we had kept a closer eye on things and taken the time to complete proper testing before implementing the system. This was a major setback. As Claire Saad recalls:

An order would come in from Macy's, and the system in Vermont would assign it to a particular rack. Then, another order would come in from the same customer, and the system would put another two units on a rack in a different part of the warehouse. When it was time to ship, where were the

14.2 Ronny, I love you! Ronny Wurtzburger and me in the Montreal showroom, 1991.

Macy's units? They'd be in different parts of the warehouse, but the computer would only recognize some of them. So we were short-shipping, to the point where some customers would only get ten per cent of their order. It was a disaster.

Ronny Wurtzburger would call and say, "This company is out of control." Customers were calling and demanding their missing suits. At the same time, we were trying to add a new fully integrated software system, SAP, which depended on the inventory system to function properly; nothing was working. Once we finally solved the inventory software problems, we were able to implement the sophisticated SAP system. Those two computer systems became the foundation of our success to this day.

The computer catastrophe was far from our only problem. More crucial to our long-term market position and our branding was the fact that our factory quality had started to slide. We were having problems with sleeves twisting, and the garments looked terrible. I remember one of our salesmen saying at a meeting, "At least if the product was good, shipping late would be OK." But the product didn't fit, we didn't ship on time, *and* we short-shipped. Everything seemed to be going wrong. I think we had stopped paying attention to the factory because it had always been the company's strength.

Our enormous and rapid growth had put a huge strain on our management team. Although I was semiretired, I was certainly aware of what was going on at Peerless and had waited long enough for our plant manager to fix the problem. I had to get involved again to find a new designer who could fix the quality of our garments. Our plant manager was annoyed by my involvement and thought his future was in jeopardy, so he decided to leave the company. Joel and I then promoted our head mechanic, a long-term employee who had been with me when we built the factory, and made him the new plant manager. It wasn't easy to find a designer who knew the engineered coat system. After trying two unsuccessfully, I finally found an American named Pat Caruso who had experience with the engineered suit and would be able to fix the product. I thought he was a perfect fit, but the new plant manager did not involve Pat or make him part of the team.

At this time, a new opportunity arose when we were given the chance to buy a Toronto-based suit manufacturing company called Westin Road Manufacturing, owned by my friend Paul Mancini. Westin had some SME quota and could make some of our higher-priced labels. We sent our plant manager and old designer to see the factory. After their visit, Paul called me and said, "Who are those two clowns you sent? They don't even know how to hold a jacket to check if the sleeve is hanging properly." I told him, "I know it's a problem, and I'm working on it."

While Joel and I knew that changes in our Montreal management had to be made, we couldn't agree on a solution. The future of the company was at stake.

15

Back in the Saddle

Nine months had passed and the problems at Peerless still weren't solved. Joel and I continued to have different opinions about how to ensure the long-term survival of the company. The challenge was to keep our father-son relationship intact while making changes to the management team. At the end of the Peerless factory's summer vacation in 2000, and after a very sensitive, emotional, and sincere discussion, Joel decided to leave the Peerless management team. He had been handling all our family's finances and investments as well as carrying out his duties at Peerless. The "family office" was becoming a more important responsibility, and he decided to take it on full-time. I was disappointed to see my son leave, but we agreed that it was the best decision at that time. I hadn't expected that to happen, but I also thought that our relationship was more important than anything else. Before leaving, Joel said, "Dad, you built the company, you know how to fix it." After eight years of semiretirement, I had to return to leading the company full-time.

The first thing Joel and I did was call the bank to let them know what we had decided. The bank understood and was very happy that we had made that decision together. The next important thing I had to do was tell Ronny, our American president, who had been responsible to Joel on the day-to-day activities of the company. When I told him about Joel's departure Ronny wasn't shocked, because he knew that major changes had to be made. He said, "Welcome back, but who's going to watch me?" I replied, "Ronny, I'm back in the saddle. I will watch everything."

This event was as tremendous a change in my life as it was for Peerless. I hadn't anticipated Joel leaving or my return to running the company. Having worked most of my life towards building Peerless, I knew what I had to do and I had to act quickly. The first thing I did was tell our plant manager that I was coming back to work, and he'd be responsible to me from now on. He'd been with Peerless for twenty years as head mechanic, but was now struggling in his new position as plant manager. He said that if Joel was leaving, he'd rather leave Peerless as well. Next, I called in our head designer and told him that Joel and the plant manager had both decided to leave; he then said, "If they're leaving, I'm leaving!" I had just lost three key men in the company, but at that moment, rather than being disappointed, I saw new opportunities on the horizon.

The same day, before lunch, Paul Mancini, the owner of the factory we had agreed to buy in Toronto (Westin Road Manufacturing), arrived at the front door of our Montreal building. I told him there had been some major changes and that Joel, our plant manager, and our head designer were leaving. He said, "Is there anything I can do to help?" I invited him to attend our lunch meeting, which I thought might help clarify what was going on.

At lunch, I explained the situation to our other key people, Claire Saad and our new designer, Pat Caruso. When Claire and Pat heard that Joel was leaving, they both told me they wanted to leave. It seemed like everyone loved Joel and didn't want me back! I'd had a strong connection with Claire from the minute Joel hired her, and I wanted her to stay. As for Pat, I knew he could take over the design responsibilities right away, and there was no way I was going to let him leave. In order to keep them, I said, "No, you're not leaving; you are both going to be vice-presidents." Claire was, at that point, intimidated by me, and stated she wouldn't like working for me. Again, I told her, "You're a vice-president now; let's see what happens going forward."

By the end of that meeting, I had made Claire the senior VP of production and distribution, and Pat Caruso the VP of design.

Since the fabric buying was done in Montreal, I named Darrell Henson VP of merchandising. As I became familiar with what was going on in the company, I realized that doing our merchandising in Montreal wasn't very efficient. So a week later, I decided it would be a good idea to move it to New York under Ronny's supervision. Darrell had just bought a new home and didn't want to move to New York, so he decided to leave as well. However, Westin Road had a merchandising manager who was a New Yorker and wanted to move back home anyway. We hired him. This immediately solved problems in communication between Montreal and New York, and enabled Ronny to oversee all the merchandising.

The big question that remained was what to do with our new integrated computer software system, SAP. We hadn't gone live with the system yet, but there was no turning back as we'd spent so much time and money to get to where we were. After many meetings and discussions, we decided to stay with it. It took a few more months until we went live on Easter weekend in 2001, coincidentally, the same long weekend we had moved the factory in 1988. I thought that was a good sign. Looking back, I'm very thankful that Joel had the vision to introduce SAP to the company as it became the support system for our success today.

During the two-year period that involved the installation of the SAP computer system, key managers like Claire had to be isolated from the day-to-day operations of the company. The software wasn't designed for the men's tailored clothing industry, and Claire had to customize it to our needs. I had to get Claire back into the daily operations of the company as soon as possible. Going live with SAP allowed her to return to the management of production, inventory, and shipping, which was desperately needed. She quickly realized there was a major inventory problem in Vermont. We had rented another warehouse for our customers' returns. There were more than 900,000 units in that warehouse, and we didn't know what their sizes, styles, colours, etc. were. There were hundreds of boxes stacked one on top of another, and there were even some suits that had been returned in shoeboxes.

This is when I realized that Ronny had been selling goods with the understanding that some customers could return the merchandise at the end of the season. Nothing is worse in business than merchandise being returned. So I told him, "No more returns. We would rather give a credit note to the retailer than take the goods back." I had total confidence and trust in Ronny and told him to make the best possible deal with the retailers. I knew that any discount would be better than having the goods back in our warehouse at the end of the season. I had learned a long time before that a shipping room must be one way only; it cannot have a revolving door.

In management meetings over the next few days, we realized that some of the preparation work we were doing in the Vermont warehouse should be brought back to Montreal. Fortunately, we were able to rent space in the building next to our parking lot at 8800 Pie-IX Boulevard, and moved the ticketing, tagging, matching, and prepacking there. That saved us money, since the Canadian dollar was still worth a low seventy cents US and labour was more available in Montreal. We were able to sort out and refurbish the entire inventory, and Ronny sold it all to our loyal discounters.

However, many of our regular customers were reducing their orders because they had lost confidence in our quality and delivery, which meant we could no longer keep our factory going at full production. We had to lower production to a minimum. We also had to introduce lower prices to cover overhead expenses and keep the factory going. Pat helped fix the quality and fit of our suits as well as reorganizing the quality managers in the factory very quickly and, as a result, Ronny started getting fewer and fewer complaints. Slowly but surely, Ronny proved to our customers that our new product was better than ever and our fill rates went back to ninety-nine per cent.

I knew I needed help with external relations, including the work I was doing with government relations in Ottawa, Quebec, and Montreal, and in our continued fight with the textile industry (we were still working to permanently remove duties from textiles not made in Canada). I learned that my long-time friend Elliot Lifson was available. Fighting with the textile industry required a professional, and Elliot fit the bill since he was a lawyer and an MBA. He would also be able to help the entire apparel industry with government relations at every level: municipal, provincial, and federal.

I named Elliot vice-chairman, and he has done an unbelievable job over the last sixteen years, speaking on behalf of the apparel industry across Canada as well as for Peerless Clothing. He is the president of the Canadian Apparel Federation (CAF) and continues to promote the industry as well as informing the government on how the industry should be rationalized between imports and domestic manufacturing. Since the fashion textile industry has almost disappeared in Canada, we have had the duty removed permanently on almost all imported textiles. As a result, certain sectors of the apparel industry are still able to operate domestically.

The major benefit of our SAP computer system is that it provides an entirely new way of managing our finances, sales, distribution, planning, and purchasing, as well as the way each department interacts with each other. After about two months, I realised our CFO wasn't familiar with the SAP system, and that he wasn't a good fit anymore for our management team. This resulted in his departure, and we promoted one of his assistants, a street-smart numbers guy named Tony Nardi, who was already working on the design for the SAP system. Tony had always impressed me, and I made him our new VP of finance.

SAP also required us to change our management style, as the information it provided led us to increased efficiency. We changed the way we handled our credit, our general ledgers, our customers, and our financial controls. Pierre Boucher, who had been a consultant when we were installing SAP, became VP of technology. Since he knew the system inside out, he was a great addition to the team.

Going to Israel every year, studying Jewish philosophy and Jewish principles at the Shalom Hartman Institute, always inspired me to think for myself and be responsible for my own destiny. After that year's annual study week in Jerusalem, I came back with new ideas for further reorganization of my management team. Knowing that I had too many people reporting to me, I called a meeting and introduced my new concept. I wrote four titles on four index cards: *Inside* (operations), *Outside* (sales), *Money* (finances), and *Factory* (manufacturing) and handed them out to my team.

Claire was working alongside Ronny and was responsible for all American orders. I realized that she was really doing the job of an operations manager, so I gave her the *Inside* card. I gave the *Money* card to Tony Nardi, the *Outside* card to Ronny, and the *Factory* card to Pat Caruso. I wanted our key managers to understand that, regardless of their titles, every department depended on the others in order to function properly. The cards helped them understand what their responsibilities were without fancy titles, and reinforced the idea of working as a team. Eventually, that idea led to the new management structure of the company, which is still in place today. I always tried to keep it simple. After a couple of years, Claire became the chief operating officer (COO), we eliminated the position of VP operating officer, and Tony became the CFO, since he was already doing that job.

As our product improved over the years, Ronny acquired more designer labels and we became even bigger. At our peak production, we had more than 3,000 sewing operators producing all our sales from our factory in Montreal. Of all the licences Ronny acquired for Peerless, some of the biggest names are Ralph Lauren, Calvin Klein, Donna Karan, Michael Kors, and Sean John.

Ronny and I decided to base our future growth on these international designer labels rather than building our own brand. This was a critical decision, and we both knew the potential danger. When you license a label but don't own it, there is always the possibility of the owner taking the licence back and managing it on his own. This has always been a fear of mine. My idea was to make Peerless so efficient and strong in marketing, merchandising, sales, and operations that we would become indispensable to our licensors. I like to think that we have built an unbreakable and mutually beneficial partnership with our licensors.

The market also influenced us to make this decision, because sales at retail are very much influenced by the popular international labels. These days, even if a suit is identical to a less expensive "no name" brand, consumers tend to purchase the one from the known designer. We thought about designing our own Peerless label, but after meeting with a Madison Avenue advertising firm and learning what would be involved, we decided not to go in that direction. I'm not a marketer. It's not in my personality. I'd rather be more flexible and be a licensee of many international labels. In retrospect, our decision to sign licence contracts with known international labels was definitely the right one.

16

Ralph Made Me Do It:
Are We an Importer or a Manufacturer?

In the early part of the twenty-first century, retailers and consumers demanded lower prices. Every department store was becoming a discounter. Since there had been no increase in the NAFTA quota, even Peerless had to compete with low-priced imports, since it seemed like all our competitors were importers.

Our biggest label at that time was "Chaps by Ralph Lauren." After more than a decade of manufacturing their suits, we were told by the Ralph Lauren company they were taking their name off the label and it would now read only "Chaps." This was because they Wanted Chaps suits to be marketed in competition with the lower-priced imports. We complained to the Ralph Lauren company that we couldn't manufacture the suits in Montreal for the price point they wanted Chaps to sell for at retail. We didn't want to become an importer, but to keep the label we had to find a way to source the suits at a lower retail price point; we had to follow the market.

Ronny and I knew this meant another change for Peerless. From 1919 to 2003 everything had been made in our Montreal factory. But now, given Ralph Lauren's new direction for Chaps, we couldn't compete with imports, and so we had to join the club.

Not knowing anything about sourcing imports, we considered purchasing an established import company. One of our competitors was available, and we negotiated a purchase price to buy the company after a nine-month engagement period. After one month working with the owner of the company, I realized that I could

CHAPS

RALPH LAUREN

16.1a The original Chaps label, featuring Ralph Lauren's name.

develop my own management team at Peerless and grow the import business on my own. I paid him the penalty we'd agreed on and walked away. Then I hired a consultant for six months to help train our management team, since there was a significant amount of paperwork, rules, and regulations to contend with.

Importing finished garments would require us to source from factories around the world. For more than fifteen years, Raffi Ajemian had provided me with technical support for the constant improvement of our product. I found out that Raffi wanted to leave his company and move to New York. He knew almost all the men's suit manufacturers around the world since he had been servicing them with fusibles, interlinings, and technical support for many years. I asked him to join our management team at Peerless Clothing International. He became our executive VP of designing and sourcing, working out of our New York office. Raffi put us in touch with many of the factories he had been dealing with and we quickly found a source to produce the product that would satisfy the new market position for the Chaps label.

Knowing this would affect the future of our factory, I called a meeting of all our factory employees in the cafeteria. I ended up having to hold three meetings of one thousand employees each, because not everyone could fit into the cafeteria at the same time. I told our people, "I tried to avoid being an importer, but at this point I have no choice." Out of the three meetings, only one person asked a question. "Mr Segal, we're worried about you. What

16.1b The new Chaps label.

are you going to do?" I didn't know what to answer; I just knew the company had to keep going. The workers knew I had tried everything I could to keep our Montreal factory operating. I felt badly that we would have to shrink our factory because I knew it would lead to layoffs, and that was the last thing I wanted. The factory employees understood, and we very slowly reduced our production. Between natural turnover and temporary layoffs, over a period of a year and a half, we reduced our factory work-force by about 1,500 employees. We've since rehired many of those employees.

Manufacturing offshore not only opened the door to lower costs but also made Peerless more competitive and versatile. Our potential for growth became enormous because of our access to multiple factories around the world. That allowed us to manufacture many different men's wear products at every price point in the market. It also enabled Ronny to sign more licence agreements with designer labels and increase our sales volume significantly. We quickly became not only the biggest manufacturer but also the biggest importer of men's tailored clothing. Manufacturing offshore was not only determined by cost; there was also the question of labour availability in Montreal to meet the increased demand in sales. We now deal with close to twenty of the best factories around the world for different price levels and different tailored men's wear products.

We have slowly built relationships with the factories Raffi has introduced us to. The knowledge and expertise from our Montreal factory has enabled us to exchange ideas and systems and ensure

16.2 Raffi and I visiting a potential factory in India, 6 December 2004.

that our imported products remain consistent with the quality standards we have worked so hard to create over the years. When Raffi started, he and I would travel together, meeting with the owners of potential factories. I wanted to be involved, in order to better understand the business of imports and to ensure that our import factories were a success. Today we have local teams stationed in each country we manufacture in, as well as a team of inspectors who travel to each factory around the world on a regular basis, verifying quality and delivery schedules. Although we have never invested in offshore factories, we have put methods in place to ensure that our quality standards and design requirements are met, so all Peerless garments regardless of where they are made have the same high quality standards. We also put emphasis on building tremendous relationships with the factories we deal with.

Our main labels, Ralph Lauren and Calvin Klein, included over-coats and topcoats, which we had been sublicensing to another company, owned by Jeff Weintraub, who is now a very close friend. Once we became an importer of finished garments it made sense to purchase that company, releasing us from our sublicensing contract and adding to our Peerless sales.

One of the largest American manufacturers of men's suits, Hart Schaffner Marx, had a problem competing with imports and, after being reorganized for the second time, approached us with a new opportunity. Peerless would become the sales and marketing agent for their "Made in America" higher-priced suit label, manufactured in their Chicago factory. We would handle their sales and marketing from our New York office and showroom. This strategic alliance gave us more exposure and allowed us to tap into a new market of higher-priced retailers to promote and expand our other international labels.

In 2006 we had the opportunity to form a new division: boys' tailored clothing. A salesman with expertise in that industry became available, and Ronny hired him. That business has grown significantly over the last ten years and we now also sublicense boys' shirts and ties to most of our US department stores. The same year, we purchased the assets of a company called "Tallia." This made us the owners of our own label for the first time, which meant we were not only able to control the direction of the brand but also sublicense other products like shirts, neckwear, sweaters, and men's accessories under the Tallia label. There is tremendous potential to promote the Tallia brand in the future as a licensor, which is almost a separate business in itself.

In the last ten years, we have doubled our sales volume. This required us to move our New York sales office to a much larger space at 641 Lexington Avenue. Each label has its own identity and must look unique, and each requires separate merchandising and its own sales team. Each line changes every season; department-store buyers are in our New York office on a regular basis and they expect the lines to look fresh and new, not just in terms of fabric but also in styling and models. Textile mills from around the world regularly meet at our New York office with our merchandisers to show their new fabric lines. As well, suit manufacturers and contractors from around the world gather in our New York office on a regular basis to introduce new sourcing opportunities. Today our New York sales office is represented by the greatest sales team in the industry, all under the age of fifty.

For the last fifteen years, Peerless has held an annual golf tournament in White Plains, New York. We invite all of our customers and our suppliers, together with our sales team, to the tournament. It's a great way to thank them for their loyalty, and offers them a chance to relax and build partnerships with our sales team.

Under the leadership of our Director of Distribution, Ramesh Bansee, we have also been investing continually in expanding our warehouse and distribution center in St Albans, Vermont, transforming it into a state-of-the-art, computer-controlled facility of more than one million square feet employing close to 500 people. This distribution center, with our integrated inventory system, allows us to service our customers more efficiently, and separates us from our competitors. "Electronic data interchange" (EDI) is a system that enables us to restock our customers' inventory in key items without human intervention. Each time a garment is sold at retail and a barcode is scanned, the EDI system automatically generates new demand from our warehouse. We then satisfy this demand on a weekly basis, replenishing the customer's inventory within a forty-eight-hour turnaround. We do this fifty-two weeks of the year with a ninety-nine-per-cent fill rate, accounting for roughly half our total sales volume of more than a million garments a month. Our ability to do this successfully makes us indispensable to our retailers and, in turn, our licensors.

We also support the dot com businesses of some of our customers by shipping orders directly from our warehouse to the end consumer. So, for example, a man in Nebraska buys a suit online from a major department store, the order comes directly to our warehouse, and the suit is shipped to the purchaser without the department store's involvement. We do this tens of thousands of times per month.

The fact that we've maintained our factory in Montreal has given us a tremendous advantage over our competitors who are

16.3 Peerless Clothing factory on Boulevard Pie-IX, 2016.

only importers, not manufacturers. Because of the distance and long delivery times between our Asian contractors and our North American customers, we maintain a Montreal factory employing approximately one thousand operators. Our factory in Montreal gives our design and production teams the ability to innovate, creating and producing original designs and thousands of samples every season for our customers. We can also complete rush orders and serve our customers' specific needs and requests. We have learned to rationalize production, both domestic and import, in order to develop the right product for the right price, to be delivered at the right time.

Our Montreal factory has been upgraded, and now has the capacity to make a higher quality "half-canvas" garment sold to customers at the higher price point. Every day, our trucks take the Montreal production to our Vermont distribution centre. Since the trucks would otherwise return empty, we take that opportunity to transport imported garments requiring quality touch-ups or repairs from Vermont back to our Montreal factory. This way, we make the best use of the expertise and labour at our Montreal facility. The next day, the garments are returned to Vermont, and because the merchandise is in bond, no duty is paid on the garments as the trucks cross the border in either direction. All of the above defines our unique competitive advantage.

Since Peerless is primarily in the international labels business, there is always insecurity that one of those labels could be taken back by the licensor. By continually focusing on customer service and investing in state-of-the-art technology, we hope to build a strong bond with our licensors and customers. As far as I know, none of our competitors can provide the level of service we can, and hopefully the relationship with our licensors will continue to grow. Over the years, we've strengthened our management team, inventory system, factory, and our warehouse in St Alban's to be the best in the business.

At the time of this writing our story isn't over. We are now planning a major investment in our St Albans warehouse buildings and systems to accommodate future growth. We are planning to add another 300,000 to 400,000 square feet of space to our existing buildings, and we will be adding a state-of-the-art sorter to our warehouse as well. This expansion will cost more than twenty-two million dollars and will create many more jobs in St Albans. As this book nears completion, we have signed a contract to license another major label: Tommy Hilfiger, as of 1 January 2018. Fortunately, in today's fashion climate, men continue to buy and wear beautiful tailored suits. At the end of our last fiscal year, both sales and profits were going strong, and our management team is very positive about our future.

In 2016 I turned eighty-three years old, and am in good health as far as I know. I am still doing the same thing I have been doing for the last sixty-five years: manufacturing popular-priced men's tailored clothing. For the last ten years, I've been discussing a succession plan with Ronny. It's something that's crossed my mind many times. Succession is one of the toughest challenges a privately owned family business can face. The main goal is to find someone who embodies the founder's mission and values long after he is gone, but that's not always easy to do.

People from the business world tell me that nothing lasts forever, and I should sell the company. We have considered hiring

16.4 My management team, at an annual meeting in Florida, 2006.
Left to right, back row, David Poronovich, Tony Nardi, Pat Caruso, David
Wolpin, Raffi Ajemian, and in the front, Ronny Wurtzberger, Claire Saad,
and me.

someone eventually to replace Ronny and me. A great business
leader has to know every side of the company, and hiring an outsider would mean taking the time to train that person properly.
Since my children aren't part of the day-to-day operations of the
business, I've been wondering who would be able to rise to the
occasion and continue growing Peerless.

At the Peerless 2015 annual winter retreat, a two-day meeting
with my key executives which takes place in Florida, Ronny made
a suggestion that was immediately approved by everyone. Douglas
Raicek, my eldest grandson, a graduate of Dartmouth College with
an MBA from Harvard, started working in our New York office
right after Labour Day weekend in 2014. Ronny suggested custom-
izing a two-year program that would enable Douglas to become
part of our future management team. Since Douglas had shown
great potential and an understanding of the company in the few
months he'd been employed by us, Ronny thought he would be the

perfect person to lead Peerless into the future. Douglas was born on my mother's *yahrzeit* on the ninth day of Iyar. To me, that is a good luck sign.

For many reasons, in January 2010, after nineteen years of marriage, Leanor and I decided to divorce. After two failed marriages, I was determined to remain single, but that was not meant to be. My long-range plan had to change the day I met a very special woman, Emmelle, who I did not want to lose. She became Mrs Segal (the third) within a year. Third time's a charm, and I'm so blessed to have her by my side.

So much has improved since the day I started working in the Peerless factory. The federal government's Lumley Task Force was formed to help the textile and apparel industries work together. The CTI and apparel industries are now represented under the same umbrella in the Canadian Apparel Federation (CAF) office. It took forty years, but I knew it would eventually happen. Now we make sure that apparel and textiles speak with one voice.

We were also assisted by our federal government in phasing out the duty on most fabrics. When the removal of tariffs came into effect in 2010, it was applied retroactively for one year and all apparel manufacturers received a refund from the federal government for the duty we all paid during that period. All my efforts to eliminate tariffs on components for men's fine tailored clothing benefitted not only Peerless, but the entire men's tailored clothing industry in Canada, though, to be honest, I never got a thank you from anyone. It just shows they never realized how much work I had been doing on their behalf.

The provincial government's disbandment of the Joint Committee system helped to keep the industry flexible. As president of the MCMA, I believe that I was instrumental in that decision. Our Teamsters local understands that to compete in this market we must stay up to date and change with the times, and we are both growing and benefitting together; so are our employees, who still have paid Jewish holidays.

Through the years, Peerless has learned to rationalize its imports and domestic production. This is key because our factory is a repository of knowledge, and keeping it in operation has been an important aspect of our continued growth and success. Yes, the world has changed, but after sixty-five years in this great industry I'm still, at every opportunity, checking to see if the collars fit. I've certainly spent my life looking for that one more improvement to our product: a new fabric, trimming, an adjustment to the pattern to make the fit more comfortable, or a shell fabric to give the customer better value. I still do this, even today, as an advisor to my team of experts. My path with Peerless was "tailor made." It *suited* me just fine.

On the cusp of Peerless's one hundredth anniversary, which will take place in 2019, I'm glad to say that we are still "Canada's best value in clothing," the same slogan we had when I started at Peerless in 1951. As I finish writing this book, I have the greatest management team I could ever have hoped for. With the company in their hands, Peerless is sure to continue.

Afterword

ELLIOT LIFSON, VICE-CHAIRMAN, PEERLESS CLOTHING

On first reading Alvin Segal's most interesting story, you might get the feeling that his life is governed by a "seat of the pants" approach to management and that he makes decisions on the fly. If you believe that, then you might also believe that Alvin's hearing impediments prevent him from knowing what people around him are saying.

I've known Alvin for more than forty years, and he really hasn't changed all that much. His main philosophy is to look forward, never back. Alvin has the ability to feel the pulse of the environment around him and the rare willingness to acknowledge a bad decision and change it if he's made a mistake. He delegates and encourages people to make their own decisions. This has helped him develop a management team that is not afraid to take risks.

As his company grew, Alvin developed and encouraged a competent young management team to take over and run the day-to-day operations of Peerless. He is supportive and really doesn't micro-manage. He loves what he does and receives immense satisfaction in seeing how the company evolves. Sometimes he is overwhelmed by its size and doesn't know all the little things that go on as he did when the company was smaller, but he has an innate feel for the business.

Alvin's business sense is matched by his love for the industry, which gave him opportunities he never dreamed possible. That has inspired him to share his experience as best he can, and has driven him to work on enhancing the competitiveness of the apparel industry. To this day, he is an active executive of the

Canadian Apparel Federation. Alvin's efforts in the negotiation of the FTA and NAFTA are legendary. He was also one of the longest sitting members of the SAGIT (Sectorial Advisory Group for International Trade).

Along with his sense of responsibility to the apparel industry, Alvin has a sense of responsibility to his community. He has never forgotten where he came from or that his roots are Jewish, and the Jewish community benefits from his support. The Jewish Public Library and its great Yiddish archives, the Jewish day school system, and the Jewish Studies Program at McGill University are all recipients of Alvin's generosity.

His philanthropy includes the Jewish General Hospital, which serves everyone in Montreal and throughout Quebec regardless of religious belief. The Jewish General Hospital means a lot to Alvin because it was there that his mother received wonderful care during one of the most difficult periods of his life, and of course hers. He never forgot this, and it resulted in one of his most important legacies: the Segal Comprehensive Cancer Centre at the Jewish General Hospital. The Segal family maintains an ongoing relationship with the hospital through their support of the McGill University Chair in Molecular Oncology and are involved in year-round fundraising activities for Hope and Cope (care for cancer patients and their families) – even Peerless employees are involved each year in the walk for cancer.

Besides his concerns for health and education, Alvin's love of Jewish and Yiddish culture led him to establish the Segal Centre for Performing Arts, which has become the center of Montreal's English theatre community, ably led by Lisa Rubin, artistic and executive director. With Alvin's support, the theatre has evolved and extended far beyond Yiddish theatre, into music, dance, and professional theatrical productions. Alvin not only supports the theatre financially but also through personal involvement. At opening nights, you will always find Emmelle and Alvin in their usual seats. Alvin also records some of the shows with his own video camera.

In 2010, because of the lives touched and charitable work achieved through his foundation, the Jewish Community Foundation honoured Alvin with the title "Man of the Year." This honour is given each year to extraordinary leaders, innovators, and philanthropists who have enhanced the Montreal Jewish community with their passion and acts of giving.

Canada, Quebec, and Montreal have not ignored Alvin's contributions to industry, health, and culture. In 2002 he was named a Member of the Order of Canada (CM) for his leadership in industry. Then in 2010, for his contributions to his community in health, education, and culture, he was elevated to Officer of the Order of Canada (OC).

Alvin's home province of Quebec also recognised his contributions to industry and the community by inducting him into a distinguished group of Quebecers, as an officer of L'Ordre National du Québec (OQ) in 2011.

Not to be outdone, Montreal has also honoured Alvin. In 2014 the Academy of Great Montrealers (now called the Order of Montreal/L'Ordre de Montréal) named him a "Grand Montréalais." The award was bestowed by Montreal's mayor, Denis Coderre, and Michel Leblanc, the president and CEO of the Montreal Board of Trade who described the award as shining the "spotlight on those who through their talent, commitment and generosity, have helped make Montreal what it is today."

In 2014 Prime Minister Stephen Harper granted Alvin the Prime Minister's Volunteer Award for Business Leader for the region of Quebec. Alvin and Peerless were together recognized for forward thinking and voluntary contributions to the community. Here's how the government described Alvin's contribution:

Alvin Segal has a passion and love for his company and industry, and makes sure to contribute not only to the welfare of the industry, but also to anything that can benefit the whole community. Mr Segal has encouraged government, corporations and other individuals towards philanthropic activity in support of health, culture and education.

Peerless Clothing has also developed training programs that have helped newcomers to Canada take up production jobs. The unionized workforce at Peerless brings together over sixty cultural communities, making it both the largest and most diverse workplace in the industry.

One should not ignore the importance of Israel in Alvin's life. Over the past thirty-five years, while travelling to Israel, he became acquainted with the Shalom Hartman Institute in Jerusalem. During his yearly (or sometimes twice yearly) visits to his sister and her family, Alvin started studying Jewish philosophy. Studying at the Shalom Hartman Institute (SHI) brought his knowledge of Judaism to a higher level, and Alvin always returns from his trips with great ideas and new perspectives. As Alvin says, his studies at SHI have influenced the way he lives and runs his business. He believes it has made him a better person, and his financial support for the institute has grown through the years as well. When the SHI campus was built, Alvin became one of its founding members, and his donations led to the construction of the Alvin Segal Library and the Alvin Segal Beit Midrash. Through the years, his involvement with the institute led to Alvin's appointment as president of the Canadian Friends of the Shalom Hartman Institute (CFSHI).

In May 2015, Alvin became the Scopus Award honouree; Alvin says it was the most unexpected and humbling of all the accolades he has received. The Scopus is the highest honour presented by the Canadian Friends of Hebrew University (HU) of Jerusalem and is described as a tribute to "a visionary business leader, an inspirational philanthropist and overall great man." A dinner reuniting friends, family members, and colleagues from across the world was held at Shaar Hashomayim Synagogue in Montreal. During the event, the president of HU said, "Every community needs an Alvin Segal." It was a statement that moved Alvin deeply.

Anybody close to him knows he has never enjoyed giving speeches in front of crowds, but, with years, he has become a little better at the delivery though he always tends to keep it short. For this event, Alvin thought it would be a great idea to include his wife, Emmelle, in the ceremony. He decided to write a "Thank you" speech that would include both of them, and says that standing in front of everybody with her by his side made the evening that much more memorable for him.

As part of the Scopus, Hebrew University held a ceremony in Jerusalem, and during it the university bestowed on Alvin an honorary doctorate – Philosophiae Honoris. Now Alvin's official title would be changed to Alvin C. Segal, oc, oq, PhD (hc). Alvin was surrounded by family, including his wife, daughter Renee, and his sisters Harriet and Connie for the ceremony, a fact that he says meant the world to him.

Alvin's greatest love is his family: his wife, children, grandchildren, his sisters and their families. Alvin loves people, and I have witnessed over the years his fondness for all individuals, no matter their rank or stature. He likes nothing better than to strike up a conversation with a complete stranger, and have them talk about themselves.

I have also witnessed the Alvin Segal who does not want to give speeches morph into one of the greatest orators at meetings in Ottawa in front of ministers and industry executives in discussions related to the protection of our fashion sector, such as one of his greatest battles, the reduction on textile tariffs on those fabrics not produced in Canada.

When it comes to his success, nobody is more surprised than Alvin. He never intended to become the boss or the owner of Peerless; it just happened that way. He just wanted to keep doing his job, and never planned to remain at Peerless for over sixty-five years. All of this would not have been possible without the support of his family, a most capable Peerless management team, and, of course, his passion for this great industry, a passion which allows him to get up every morning and to love what he does every single day.

A.1 His Excellency the Right Honourable David Johnston invested me as an Officer of the Order of Canada, 2010.

A.2 In 2011 Premier Jean Charest honoured me with Officer of the Order of Quebec.

A.3 Dr Gerald Batist, Chair of the Segal Cancer Centre, my wife Emmelle, and me photographed in one of the laboratories of the new Segal Cancer Centre in 2011.

A.4 Lisa Rubin and me at the Segal Centre following the opening night performance of *The Producers: A New Mel Brooks Musical*, in Yiddish, June 2016.

Organizations Supported

Some of the major organizations that the Alvin Segal Family Foundation supports:

Ben Gurion University, Israel
Bishop's University, Sherbrooke, Quebec
Brian Mulroney Institute for Government, St Francis Xavier University, Nova Scotia
Centraide du Grand *Montréal*
Concordia University, Montreal
Conseils des Arts de Montréal
Federation CJA in support of Israeli causes, Montreal
Fondation Communautaire Canadienne-Italienne du Québec
Fondation de la Mode de Montréal
Fondation de L'Hôpital Maisonneuve-Rosemont, Montréal
Fraser Institute, Canada
Friends of Israel Defence Forces, USA
Hebrew University, Israel
Jewish Community Federation, Montreal
Jewish Community Foundation, Montreal
Jewish Public Library, Montreal
JGH Hope and Cope, Montreal
Juvenile Diabetes Research Foundation, Canada
Maccabi Canada, Ontario
McGill Head and Neck Cancer Institute, Montreal
McGill University Jewish Studies Program, Montreal

Montreal Holocaust Memorial, Montreal
Mount Sinai Hospital Foundation, Montreal
MUHC – Children's Hospital, Montreal
MUHC – Shriner's Hospital, Montreal
National Arts Centre, Ottawa
National Holocaust Monument, Ottawa
Orchestre Métropolitain de Montréal
Orchestre Symphonique de Montréal
Shalom Hartman Institute, Israel
The Segal Centre for the Performing Arts, Montreal
The Segal Comprehensive Cancer Centre at the Jewish General
    Hospital, Montreal
The Segal Recreational Centre at Congregation Shaar Hashomayim,
    Montreal, a full-size gymnasium benefitting the Akiva School
    and the community

In addition to the Alvin Segal Family Foundation's support of many organizations, Mr Segal himself acquired a piece of great historical significance to donate to Congregation Shaar Hashomayim in Montreal.

During the consecration of the synagogue in May 1860, a rare Canadian silver presentation kiddush cup was offered by the temple to Rabbi Samuel Meyer Isaacs from New York (a man of significance with ties to Abraham Lincoln and a seminal figure in the world of American Jewry), who travelled to Montreal to deliver a speech for the occasion.

One hundred and fifty-seven years later, somehow this kiddush cup found itself up for auction at Sotheby's New York. After encouragement by the congregational clergy (Rabbi Adam Scheier, Rabbi Dr Wilfred Shuchat, and Cantor Gideon Zelermyer) and his friend Rabbi Allan Nadler, Mr Segal was convinced that this kiddush cup had to return to its original home. In January 2017, bidding along with others, including the Jewish Museum of New York, Mr Segal ended up with the winning bid.

It is now at its rightful home, at Congregation Shaar Hashomayim, and might soon be displayed in a special case outside the new Segal Family Chapel.

Awards Granted

2002 Queen's Golden Jubilee Medal. For making a significant contribution to Canada.

2005 Named Honorary Fellow of the Shalom Hartman Institute, Israel, in recognition of his leadership and devotion to the vision of a Judaism that can thrive in a modern pluralistic society.

2006 Prix-Arts-Affairs de Montréal (Arts and Business category). Presented by Conseil des Arts de Montréal (Montreal Arts Council) in partnership with the Chambre du Commerce du Montréal Métropolitain (Board of Trade of Metropolitan Montreal). This is an annual award that honours members of the business community who have distinguished themselves through their support of the arts.

2010 Jewish Community Foundation "Man of the Year." Honourees are leaders, innovators, and philanthropists who have enhanced the Montreal Jewish community with their passion and acts of giving.

2011 Lifetime Achievement Award from McGill University's Desautel Faculty of Management. This award recognizes a career resulting in great achievement and a significant contribution to Canadian business and society.

2011 Award for Outstanding Philanthropist. Awarded by the Association of Fundraising Professionals for generous, long-term contributions to initiatives in healthcare, culture, and education.

2012 Queen Elizabeth Diamond Jubilee Medal. For dedicated service and contributions to peers, the community, and Canada.

2012 Fashion Division Honour. Granted by the United Jewish Appeal (UJA) Federation of New York, this award honours exceptional leadership and remarkable achievements.

2013 The Fraser Institute Founders' Award, named after founders T. Patrick Boyle and Michael A. Walker, is the Institute's highest honour. The award is presented annually to individuals in recognition of their exceptional entrepreneurial achievements, generous philanthropic endeavours, and dedication to competitive markets. These individuals are role models for the next generation of entrepreneurs and leaders.

2014 Prime Minister's Volunteer Award (PMVA) for a Business Leader for the region of Québec. An award that recognizes the exceptional contributions of volunteers, local businesses, and innovative not-for-profit organizations in improving the wellbeing of families and communities.

2014 Grand Montréalais (Great Montrealer), Economic Sector, Chambre du Commerce du Montréal Métropolitain (Board of Trade of metropolitan Montreal). Each year the Académie des grands montréalais (the academy of Great Montrealers) is proud to honour four Montreal luminaries who have distinguished themselves through outstanding contributions to the community in their respective spheres of activity, whether economic, social, cultural, or scientific.

2015 Scopus Award Honouree. The Scopus Award is the highest honour conferred by the Friends of the Hebrew University of Jerusalem. Mr Segal received the honour for being a visionary business leader, an inspirational philanthropist, and overall great man.

2015 Honorary Doctorate – Philosophiae Honoris Causa. The Hebrew University awards honorary degrees to persons who have distinguished themselves by academic or creative achievement, who have rendered outstanding service to the university, or whose activities have been of notable benefit to humanity, the State of Israel, or the Jewish people.

Index

Aberman, Sam, 128. *See also* Divco

Abony, David, 44

AFL-CIO, 166–7

Ajemian, Raffi, 111, 180–2, 187

Alexander, Bill, 87

Amalgamated Clothing Workers of America (ACWA), 33, 46, 51, 53–4, 56, 77–8, 104, 115, 125, 136, 155. *See also* sectoral union; UNITE

American Clothing Manufacturers Association (ACMA), 152–3

American Men's Clothing Manufacturers Association (AMCMA), 105

anti-Semitism, 13, 17, 21–2; attending United Church, 21

Apparel Manufacturers Institute of Quebec (AMIQ), 107, 112, 115–16, 125

Ballon, Adah, 61

Bansee, Ramesh, 184

Becker, Hillel, xix

boarding school. *See* Irving Prep School

boys' suits, 29, 60, 183

Brookfield Clothing, 100–1, 122, 140, 142. *See also* Soifer, Herman

Calvin Klein, 177, 183

Canada Hair Cloth, 57, 111

Canada's Best Value in Clothing, 28, 30, 93, 122, 189

Canadian Apparel Federation (CAF), 112, 176, 188, 190–1

Canadian government, xvii, 33, 71, 125, 129, 151–2, 175–6, 192; duty, 57, 106–10, 112–14, 127, 133, 135, 153, 164, 188; FTA, 114, 127, 135; lobby, xix, 110, 115; and Lumley, 115–17, 188; provincial, 49–52, 80, 107, 188; SAGIT, 133–5

Canadian International Trade Tribunal (CITT), 111, 113–14, 135, 153